THE SEASONS OF THE BLIND

R. C. Scriven

The Seasons of the Blind

AND OTHER RADIO PLAYS IN VERSE

British Broadcasting Corporation

Published by the
British Broadcasting Corporation
35 Marylebone High Street
London W1M 4AA

ISBN 0 563 12660 4

First published 1974

Printed in Great Britain
by Tonbridge Printers Limited, Peach Hall Works,
Shipbourne Road, Tonbridge, Kent.

Contents

The British Broadcasting Corporation are most grateful to the Yorkshire Arts Association for the grant they have kindly made towards the publication of this book.

Dedicated to the memory
of my Father and Mother
who gave me the greatest
of all gifts.

R.C.S.

The author has asked for an acknowledgement
to be made of his debt to all the producers,
casts, sound engineers and other technicians
without whom no radio would be possible,
and to whom so many writers owe so much.

Introduction

Ronald Scriven, Sunday's Child, was born near Sheffield on 21 April 1907, the first son of Jack, an engineer, and engineering ran in the family, for Ronald's grandfather founded the Leeds firm of Scriven-Crossthwaite, machine tool manufacturers, which still operates today.

One winter when his mother was ill Ronald, always an inquisitive child, was forbidden to go out by his grandmother, so watched instead the Leeds world go by on bitter days through the lifted flap of the letter-box. The inflammation of his ears which followed left him at eight nearly stone deaf—but the real damage was to his eyes which, thirty years later, became clouded by glaucoma, his sight too being lost.

It was not long after he became deaf, with his father serving in France and his mother ill, that his Uncle James boarded him and his younger brother, Neville, at Low Moor Farm at Rigton near Harrogate with Slow Joe Robinson and Iron Ann, 'hard as a nail and twice as strong' but not intentionally cruel. It was here one night after he had read the Bible to her in the kitchen as usual that she abruptly told him both his parents had died.

He was sent to Crossley's School for Orphans at Halifax where of course he could hardly hear a single teacher's voice, except perhaps Mr Robb the English Master who, taking him aside one day, gave him *The Golden Treasury* and fired his strong poetic inclination.

Managing somehow to matriculate, he left school determined to be a poet but was forced against his will into an apprenticeship with the family firm where he became 'the worst engineer in the North' and where the apprentices, kept at work during the General Strike of 1926, but having little to do, had their attention directed by the foreman to sixty tons of coke which lay in the yard. 'He shoved a shovel in our hands and told us to shift it from "thar to thar". We spent a week on the job, and were then ordered to "shift t' bugger from thar back to thar again".'

Coming of age with an inheritance of £2000, he became partner in a Sheffield firm of showcard manufacturers, printing and stapling showcards by day and writing poetry unsuccessfully by night. The business soon becoming bankrupt, he scampered off to be a journalist, working in turn for the *Yorkshire Post*, the *Yorkshire Observer* and the *Yorkshire Evening Post*. It was not, however, until eleven years after the collapse of the showcard business that he had his first literary success with the publication of a poem in *Punch*. 'I sent one in every week for sixty-three weeks and it was always sent back. Then in the sixty-fourth week there was suddenly a proof instead of a rejection slip', and for the next thirteen years he was a regular contributor over the signature 'Ratz'.

During the second World War, despite his deafness, he worked as a staff reporter for the old *Yorkshire Observer* but during the 1940s the glaucoma developed and after a series of delicate eye operations he became totally blind, saying only: 'It did sometimes seem unkind but blindness and deafness balance one another like Milton's buckets.' What his eyes saw as they clouded over became fixed for ever in his memory for 'when a man knows he will soon be blind what he looks at stays looked at'.

As he has throughout his life, he bounced back and in 1947 wrote his first radio play 'The Peacock City of P'Tzan King', and the following year 'A Single Taper', an agonising account in verse of one of the unsuccessful operations on his eyes:

Darkness may close upon my sight –
dare I then ask for inner light?
Yes, Lord, dear Lord:
because I loved
the blaze of noon,
as Milton did,
and dawn's first, paler-than-primrose glow:
if light, seen light
I must forego –
that outward, visible sign,
which we
accept from You unthinkingly
so often –
light, denied to me.
Lord, grant me, –
if this thing must be –
contentment, to keep bitterness
at bay.

And bitterness he did keep at bay for, not having the patience to learn Braille, he went in 1952 to the blind school at Torquay for 'a three-months course on how to be blind and bleeding well like it', and here he learnt to touch-type and touch-shave, and now seldom misses a whisker.

At sixty-eight he is still a free-lance journalist and an outstanding radio playwright, living with his devoted, long-suffering and often exhausted wife, Phyllis, in the country village of Thorner, near Leeds, where he can be seen tap-tapping his way from his terraced house across the main street to The Fox. He lives in some discomfort, indomitably rolling verse off his typewriter, bubbling with a lust for life, drawing on the boyhood experiences which burn in his memory, from the sights he has not seen for over twenty-five years, and from the facts and quotations stored in his remarkable mind—'I can give you Housman and Tennyson by the yard'. As well as Housman he loves T. S. Eliot, G. K. Chesterton, Tetley's Mixed (mild and bitter), Bell's Whisky and Wensleydale Blue Cheese.

Of 'The Seasons of the Blind', which was acclaimed by the Writers Guild of Great Britain when it was commissioned by the BBC to mark the centenary of The Royal National Institute for the Blind, David Wade wrote in *The Times:*

> There can rarely have been a more intensely visual programme . . . I do not remember ever to have received in sound alone so visual an impression of landscape; it was as if by some process of direct transmission the writer's vision had been implanted in my brain . . . sharp in every detail.

And of 'All Early in the April' and 'The Peacock Screamed One Morning' he wrote:

> The exceptional quality of this writing can perhaps be summed up in its power of luminous re-creation; the sounds, sights, smells, sensations, marvels and miseries of childhood became the listener's own and all with hardly a touch of sentiment or nostalgia. Mr Scriven has been deaf since the age of eight, blind for more than twenty years yet he can teach the rest of us to hear and see.

The success of 'The Seasons of the Blind' reawakened Scriven's interest in radio and he began to explore his childhood in the series of autobiographical plays in this volume, often coming to the studio for rehearsals and sitting there impassively hour after hour, with me wondering what could be going on inside that massive head. I learnt that when I wanted to communicate with him I had but to touch his arm and he came instantly alive. By speaking slowly and distinctly straight into his hearing aid, provided there was no other sound near us, it was possible to get through to him and he would reply in the high-pitched voice he had not heard since he was eight. Once when I had to ask him if he could simplify a few lines in a play, his wife read and re-read them to him over and over again, and who can blame him that the sheer frustration of not being able to see them set out upon the page burst forth in anger?

During the recording of his first autobiographical play 'All Early in the April', unable of course to see the actors, he sat holding his battered old hearing aid close up against the loudspeaker so that he could hear something of them dimly and far off. When we reached in the play the moment of his realisation of his loss of hearing and with it the memory of that agony and subsequent isolation, a tear trickled down his face—and it was not the only tear that fell in that studio that afternoon, though he can never have known this.

CHARLES LEFEAUX

All Early in the April

All Early in the April was first broadcast on BBC Radio 4 on 18 March 1970 with the following cast:

NARRATOR	*Stephen Murray*
GERTIE SCRIVEN	*Elizabeth Proud*
JACK SCRIVEN	*Kerry Francis*
CHARLES SCRIVEN	*Peter Pratt*
CLERK	*Frederick Treves*
RONALD SCRIVEN	*Sheila Grant*
GRANDMOTHER	*Kathleen Helme*
NEVILLE SCRIVEN	*Jo Manning Wilson*
TOM	*Nigel Lambert*
AUNT CISS	*Hilda Kriseman*
WILFRED KEMP	*Judy Bennet*
UNCLE HAROLD	*Leonard Fenton*

Produced by Charles Lefeaux

(Fade up, very much in the background, music—
'On hearing the first cuckoo in Spring' by Delius).

Narrator Men are defiled
'by the contagion of the world's slow stain'.
When the wind plucks, with fingers soft or sharp,
the strings of memory's Aeolian harp,
we muse, beguiled,
grope backwards through time's disasters to explain
why sight and sound, colour, taste, smell and touch
have changed so much . . . so much.
But how can a man look at the world again
through the eyes of a child?
(Human voice as cuckoo emerging from the fading music)

Cuckoo Cuckoo.

Narrator I have passed over mountains, through forest and desert places,
dwelt briefly in the wasteland's few oases:
now I halt once more, in the shade of my years, to draw breath.
(Pause)
(sombrely) To the North lies death–
how close lie its Arctic snows I cannot guess
even in my intensest loneliness.
To the East is a possible sunrise. To the West
that improbable Land of Behest,
the Tir Nan Ogh which most men seek on earth.
(sigh) Far to the South are the dim blue hills of birth,
so dear, so alien.

Cuckoo Cuckoo.

Narrator Ah, when did I first hear you, Cuckoo, when?

Cuckoo How should I know, who do not know
how long ago,
or where,
I was born, in whose nest, nor care
that my children, before they fledge their wings
will gape and murder their fosterings
and in their turn enchant the air.

Narrator Deceitful, like all magic, Go: depart,
you cheat in the green places of the mind, you illusion.

Cuckoo *(overtone of mockery)* Cuckoo.

Narrator Or are you a dream's awakening confusion
at hearing real wings start?
(*Bring in, sharply, beat of wings brushing branches*)
True wings, or phantom, take me with you, fleeing
into the April night of my forebeing,
where I lay under my mother's heart.
(*A strong, steady beat of a heart is heard*)
Prisoner in my mother's womb,
instinct with knowledge not my own
of things my ancestors had known
– threads woven on evolution's loom
in patterns of chromosome and gene –
in darkness deeper than the April night,
unseen, unseeing,
I turned my body within her body to journey towards the unguessed light.
(*Fade heart-beat*)

Gertie Jack

Jack (*instant alertness and solicitude: both are young*) Darling.

Gertie I'm frightened. I think . . . I think . . .

Jack I'll fetch the doctor.

Narrator In the false dawn's grey blink
I see my father, so young, so agitated,
running down the short, cobble-stoned street, set at an angle,
high on a black hill, with outlines indicated
vaguely above him by a firefly tangle
of setting stars and the fitful furnace-glow
cast at the sky, illuminating it
with streaks of fire from the reeking pit
of the steel city of Sheffield, far below.
(*Fade up running footsteps, against distant day-long, night-long, industrial noise, a far-off blast furnace, and beat of nasmyth hammers*)
Did he feel, as he returned
bareheaded, the little wind which used to flow
from upland Derbyshire streams and wells cool-ferned
into those dreadful hollows? Did he hear
in the dawn the first blackbird's challenge, joyous, clear?
Did he smell oncoming rain?
Did his fingers notice, elate,

the welcoming, the cold, hard iron kiss
of the latch of the garden gate?
(*Latch of gate, double footsteps, on gravel, one pair hasty, the other noticeably heavier and unhurrying*)

Jack Here we are, doctor.
(*The front door opens. Footsteps stop*)

Gertie (*upstairs*) Jack,
Mother's here – and the midwife.

Jack I'll just see how...
(*A few rushing steps upstairs*)

Doctor (*heavy, old-fashioned jocularity*) Come back.
(*The footsteps falter and come down slowly*)
Who's having this baby? You? Take a good, long walk.
(*A moan from upstairs*)

Jack (*panic*) Oh, hurry, hurry...

Doctor Pish. You're white as a stick of chalk
I prescribe a good stiff whisky, young feller-me-lad.
(*chuckle*) You'll have plenty of time to drink it, too, I may add.
(*The doctor's slow footsteps go upstairs*)

Narrator I picture my father pacing up and down,
between elation and gloom.
I see his forehead puckered in a frown,
his chin, unshaven, a golden-copper bloom
amidst the wedding furniture, the crowded
silver-framed photographs, the windows shrouded
by curtains of crimson plush.
I see him give his waxed moustache a nervous, upwards brush
as he alters his short-stepped pace
in that mid-Edwardian place,
not grand enough to be a drawing-room.
He must have looked at his father's likeness, commanding
in silver honour, the bob-fringed mantelshelf.
Charles Scriven, the ironfounder in good standing,
Worshipful Master of his Lodge and master
of Leeds Old Foundry, uprightness itself,
his eyes as unemotional as alabaster,
his profile mutton-chopped as any Guelph,
hearing –
(*Fade up the ticking of a period clock*)
and not hearing –

the sound of the clock.
In that quiet room, my father surely thought
that time had caught
and prisoned him in a cell and turned the lock.
(Hold for a few seconds the ticking clock)
I hear the singing of that pendulum,
(Fingers drum on a window-pane)
and on those window-panes
in a devil's tattoo I hear my father drum his quick, clever
draughtsman's fingers, marked by blueprint hypo stains –
(Fingers stop)
to break off, startled, spurred,
jerking his head back at the sound he heard.
(A distant little muffled wail of birth)
So was I born. In my unconsciousness
must linger, smarting, until death's redress,
life's first sensation
of light and pain, confusion and indignation –
the birthright of all flesh
trapped in the mesh
of mortality's lowliness – and exaltation.
(Music – 'The Walk to the Paradise Garden' by Delius)
(A knock on a door)

Charles *(deep, Victorian-flavoured voice)* Come in.
(Door opens)

Clerk *(Yorkshire, not subservient)*
Telegram, Mr Charles.

Charles Thank you.
(Rip, crackle of telegram. Pause)
Tell Mr James I want him.
(Pause)

James Yes, Father?

Charles Read that.
(Pause)

James It's a boy.

Charles A grandson. My grandson, James.

James Yes, Father. And my first nephew, I suppose.

Charles You sound as though you thought he'd put your nose well out of joint.

James *(testily)* Not at all. Why should he do?

Charles Because Jack's married and started a career.
James (*keeping sarcasm well restrained*) I know he has. A consulting engineer
If you please, at twenty-three.
Leeds knows you're in with Dorman, Long. Perhaps
some of those Sheffield chaps...
Charles Have a suspicion Jack's well in with me?
And what if he is, James? What if he is? So are you..
(*abruptly*) I shall make Jack a partner... in a year or two.
When you marry and give me a grandson... we shall see.
Jack thinks in his head, without words, as an engineer should.
Remember that foreman who thought the gantry crane
hadn't the safety margin to take the strain
of a fly-wheel casting – and Jack said it would?
He looked at it three ways over the edge of his thumb
and had the slings on it before he checked
its weight with the blueprints. He was right.
James By half a ton.
Charles It was enough. You're my eldest son
by ten years – and steadier. Your time will come.
(*Pause*)
Narrator All early in the April
my span of time began,
unwitting of time's hour glass
and the grains of sand which ran
or trickled, mingled with joy or tears.
All early in the April –
love, with what hopes, what fears,
guarded my gradual flowering
for two short, two long years.
This is a central mystery,
the first dawn
of conscious memory.
The small child, a newcomer
to a most foreign land,
is puzzled by the distances which yawn
from dimension to dimension,
sees things, hears sounds he cannot understand –
and then, quicksilver eager for apprehension,
stares at shapes, sharp-cut as the shadows of summer.

He crawls through labyrinths which represent
aeons before man stood upon his feet.
He has an animal awareness of keen scent,
of cold and heat.
He learns to walk –
with ah, what tears, what tension.
Lo, he can talk.
His biological clocks are soundly ticking:
he is emotional, intelligent, alive and kicking.
As all mankind learns these things, so did I.
Then why was my rising sun of dawn veiled, why,
until the first flashing ray of memory?

(*Garden birds sing*)

Ronald I jump.

(*A light thud on grass, stumble, howl*)

Bump.
Hurt kneee.
(*Child is shocked, not hurt and reacts into anger*)
Naughty grass.

(*The grass is hit*)

Smack grass, smack grass, smack grass.

Narrator Sad symbolism in the first event
I clearly recall.
Man's memory's *not* of his divine descent
but of his earthly fall.

Ronald (*sobbing*) Granpa.

Narrator As large as through a magnifying glass
I see
a giant in a grey suit and a panama hat
tilted over his eyes, half asleep in a wicker chair
in the shade of a tree.

Charles (*rather sleepily*) Sun's hot. Must have . . . I declare
he's always in mischief. Can't take my eyes off the brat.
Now what's the matter?

Ronald Granpa, Granpa. Bump.

Charles Then pick yourself up and come here.

Narrator Charles Scriven, with his children Victorianly severe,
took off his armour with me. I think he smiled
to see me heave my petticoated rump,
stagger and rush to clamber on his knee.

Charles What are you howling about? Let's look at the place.
Crying for that, eh? A big boy like you?
I'll tell you what I'll do:
(*Jingle of a bunch of keys*)
I'll make it better with this magic bunch of keys.
(*Sobs instantly subsiding*)

Ronald Mummy makes it better with a kiss.

Charles (*chuckle*) Keys are better than kisses. Give me your finger now –
not that one, this,
it's called the forefinger. I'll show you how
to open my sovereign case.

Narrator How vivid, how direct first memories are.
My nostrils smell the smoke of his cigar.
(*Bees are heard*)
I hear the hum of bees
in the tassels of the lime,
my fingers feel the silk
of my grandfather's Ascot tie,
still, drowsily, my tongue can taste the milk
as warm as the grass-heap, as close to me as my mother's arms
when she picked me up in them and said:

Gertie Bed time.

Narrator I had learned my separate identity,
my name. I had learned to crawl, to talk, to walk,
to take my small world in Sheffield as an entity
– house, garden, tree sounds, the leathery smell of the pram,
the wild excitement of a ride in a tram,
the feel of a daisy-stalk.
Then, suddenly, at three
my world exploded every boundary.
The sky remained, the sun remained the same,
But every part was different, with a new name –
each part with a new landmark:
the parade – Leeds – Potternewton Park –
and there was a world beyond this new-known world:
The Works, a place where Daddy went.
Drowsily curled in bed, I wondered what that world was like.
From far away I heard the hall clock strike...
(*A distant chime or two of the hall clock*)
(*Pause. Distant piano and then Jack singing downstairs*)

Jack . . . My old shako,
Ten, twenty, thirty, forty, fifty years ago . . .

Ronald (*now aged a bit more than three*)
(*calling*) Daddy.
(*to himself*) It's dark . . .
(*calling*) Daddy: please can I come downstairs?
(*Music, briefly, rather louder*)
Daddy . . .
(*to himself*) Jump out of bed.
(*A light, barefoot thud*)
Cold-water floor.
(*Very light bare footsteps*)
He'll hear me if I open –
(*Door opens, music louder*)
the bedroom door.
There are giants standing on the stairs . . .
(*a bit quivery*) One . . . two . . .

Giant 1 Three

Giant 2 Four

Giant 3 Five.
If you climb down the nursery stairs . . .

All giants (*fee-fo-fum style*) We'll gobble you up alive.

Ronald (*defiantly*) I've said my prayers, I've said my prayers.

Giant 1 I didn't hear 'em. Did you?

Giant 2 No.

Giant 3 None of us heard a word of 'em.

Giant 1 (*very sinister – the giants personify fears of the dark*) So . . .
we can nab 'im and nobble 'im.

Giant 2 Grab 'im and gobble 'im.

All giants Tear 'im and share 'im:
Ho, ho, ho.

Ronald (*mingled fear and determination*) Don't, don't,
don't. I *did* say my prayers.
(*An instant, very light rush downstairs. Door opens, crescendo song*)
Daddy!
(*The song and piano stop*)

Gertie (*Very coldly*) Ronald: I've told you before. Upstairs.

Ronald (*Worked up*) Shan't. Want Daddy to kiss me good night.

Jack (*Deprecating her anger in advance*) My dear . . .

Gertie (*Ignoring this*) How dare you speak to me so rudely? Come here.

Jack Don't smack him, Gertie. Of course the child was expecting . . .
Gertie Children expect too much. He needs correcting.
With the flat of my hand, when he was two,
I taught him right from wrong, not you.
With the flat of my hairbrush, now he's three,
I teach him manners – across my knee.
Jack (*Sweet reason to disguise that he can't bear to witness what he believes to be just punishment*)
Come, we're not Victorians – nay
not even Edwardians. Ronald, say
you are sorry.
Ronald (*Not sullen, but reluctant*) I'm sorry . . . Mother.
Gertie (*Very vexed with Jack*) Really, Jack.
Ronald (*Victory – and he knows it*) I've 'pologised.
Daddy, Daddy – piggy-back.
(*Footsteps go upstairs, shrieks of joy from Ronald*)
Narrator When a man tries to look through the eyes
of the child within, his double vision
has, of necessity, imprecision,
high lights confused, however fixed,
foreground, background, perspective wavering, mixed
between time now and time then.
(*A drawer is opened*)
My grandchildren whoop at this family wedding-group,
taken in July 1910.
Yet as memory strikes the chord,
this photograph, like a song from a music hall,
can pierce my heart with a sword.
There is my dear Aunt Jess, of the Welsh-gold hair,
trying to look, at eighteen, as sedate
as her elder sister the bride at twenty-eight.
There is my Uncle James, a handsome bull,
master of his dead father's house.
There are courtesy-aunts galore, provincial, dull.
My mother's mother, plump as a pear,
wise as a monkey, quiet as a mouse.
There, standing by the bride
my mother, slender, dark, dove-eyed
and as smart as the Gaiety girls.
Around the brim of her hat, a world too wide,

an ostrich feather curls.
A second before the photograph was taken
I sat at the bridegroom's feet
in three petticoats and kid boots.
Firmly foursquare on its tripod the camera stood
and the voice of my father called from under the hood:

Jack (*Muffled*) Watch for the dicky-bird!

Narrator Panic stirred the bridegroom.
Nerves made his fingers meet
in my thick curls, down to the roots,
and he dragged me half to my feet.
The camera caught my round mouth of agony,
my glance imploring heaven.
Preposterous, absurd –
but long years after
my double vision is blurred
with tears, part pain, part laughter.
(*Pause*)
(*Abruptly*) I take another tumbled, grassheap jump
to land in nineteen eleven.
It's Coronation Year.
I play with my bricks on the dining-room rug. I hear
my grandmother's voice.

Grandmother Mother's been poorly:

Ronald Is she better yet?

Grandmother I'll take you upstairs. She wants to see you, dear.

Narrator The bedroom curtains were drawn
on the cool day, the trees, the September lawn.

Gertie (*Voice much softer than usual*)
Ronald: come and look at your baby brother.
(*Pause*)

Ronald It's ugly. Did the doctor bring it, Mother?
Mother, did he find it under a gooseberry bush?
(*A fretful wail from the infant*)
Can it talk yet? Can it?

Gertie Darling, darling, hush!

Ronald Hasn't it any teeth? Is it trying to spit?
Hasn't it...

Gertie Darling, you mustn't call him 'It':
His name is Neville.

Ronald (*With certainty*) Daddy will hate him.
Grandmother Ronald! What a thing to say!
Gertie (*Laughing*) He's jealous. Aren't you. Ronald?
(*Decisively*) Take him away...
He'll learn to love his little brother.
Grandmother Of course, of course.
Narrator In my attic playroom I rode my rocking-horse.
(*The creak of a rocking-horse*)
From the narrow dormer window I could see above the trees,
leaf-laced sun reflections,
criss-crossed in all directions
danced about my own, my gay room –
but I did not ride at ease.
Ronald It's ugly. It scowls.
I hate it. It howls.
It yells. Like the devil.
I shan't call It Neville.
Shan't love it, shan't love it.
I'll pinch it. I'll shove it.
(*Rock up horse, furiously, solo, briefly*)
(*Child is conscious of ultimate sin in his use of 'she'*) She'll talk him over. Just you see.
(*In desolation*) Daddy will love It better than me.
(*The rocking-horse stops*)
Narrator When I was six-and-sixpence
and Neville two years old,
summers were greeny-golden
and winters snowy-cold.
(*Fade up the babble of children in a Christmas toyfair*)
Down in the toyfair basement
in days as dead and gone
as the terraced Hanging Gardens
which bloomed in Babylon,
Christmas was an enchantment
not Aladdin gazed upon.
Jack Stick close beside me, Ron.
Here's Monteith, Hamilton and Monteith's
The Grand Pygmalion.
Ronald (*Now rising seven*) Meccano, Meccano! Oh, look at the Eiffel Tower.

Look at the trains. The North British, The L.N.E.R.
They're green n' gold. They work by electric power,
Look at the kinematograph, look, look,
look at the horses, galloping like mad.
And oh, oh, look: a pedal motor car.
(*A sharp, toad-of-toad-hall poop-poop of horn*)
Real headlamps. Real sidelights. May I sit in it, Dad?

Jack No, you may not.

Narrator I tugged at the hand he took...
(*A final, long-drawn poooop, cut abruptly*)

Jack Behave yourself.

Narrator In a backward-glancing dream
I followed him, dragging my heels.

Jack Hello, what's this? A mountain gun-mule team.
Ingenious. Look, three of them carry the wheels,
three, the gun barrels and the last, the ammunition.
(*to himself*) Steel wire. One-sixteenth by three-eighths.
(*Aloud*) You see –
the guns can be fitted together and used to shell
the enemy's position.

Ronald (*Enthusiasm*) And knock their bloody heads off.

Jack (*Very peremptory*) Who taught you that word?

Ronald (*Extreme apprehension*) I... I don't know, Father.

Jack Don't lie to me.

Ronald The newspaper boy.
(*To divert attention*) He doesn't know how to spell.
He called me a liar when I said I could, at three.
A b.... He said he could read and write when he was two.
(*Sudden confidence*) So I called *him* a liar. We had a fight.

Jack Never, never let me hear you say that word again.
(*Off-handedly*) Who won?

Ronald He did. But only just.
It was in the hollows. In Potternewton Lane.

Jack Right. Never tell lies. You'll remember that, I trust.

Ronald I'll remember. Dad: I can beat him at taws.

Jack If Mother heard of that fight she'd have a fit.

Ronald Dad. The newspaper boy said there isn't a Santa Claus.

Jack Did he? Suppose we look for Mother and Neville,
they're going to his grotto – and yes, by Jove, that's it.
(*Fade up in distance a hurdy-gurdy playing a tune of 1913*)

Narrator Convinced the tale of Santa Claus was true,
how could one wait for Christmas?
Ronald It's *days* away.
Narrator Dusk came snow-sprinkled, hazily, grey-blue,
to curtain nursery tea-time afternoons
(*Hurdy-gurdy louder*)
Gertie Listen . . .
Ronald A tingalairy.
Gertie Playing for Lampie, with his magic wand.
(*Ronald claps his hands*)
(*The hurdy-gurdy fades*)
Narrator The lamps, along the evening avenue,
seemed to hang from the sky, beyond
the reach of Lampie's rod like gold balloons.
All my child's world was mystery, preparation,
locked cupboards, baking smells, great expectations,
events both standing still and rushing past
as the heart's pendulum swung, now slow, now fast.
A world wrapped round with life's most magic stuff.
Grandmother Ronald: would you like to fetch Grandma's muff?
Gertie (*Slight surprise*) Going out? It's Christmas Eve tomorrow night.
Grandmother (*All gentle innocence*) I'm going to see Mrs Lawn, dear. Shan't be late.
Gertie (*Very faint suspicion*) As long as you're quite sure . . .
Grandmother (*Placidly*) Quite.
Ronald Look – mint imperials.
Grandmother (*Very slightly put out: the mints are tell-tale*)
Come with me to the gate
and I'll give you both a mint imperial.
Gertie Wait . . .
Grandmother (*Firmly*) Give me your hand, Neville. Ronald, don't tug at my sleeve.
Narrator On the morning of Christmas Eve,
agog with joy,
in my dressing-gown and socks,
I whispered to the paper-boy
through the flap of the letter-box:
Ronald (*Shouting, not too loudly*) Would you like some oranges, Fred?
We've got hundreds of oranges, thousands of oranges,
millions of oranges.

Fred (*Yorkshire, highly suspicious, outside door*)
You're off yer head.
Ronald Honest Injun. Crates and crates of 'em.
You ask Anna. Hundredweights of 'em.
Granny brought them home last night, in a four-wheel cab.
She was singing.
Fred Must've been tight.
Ronald (*He hasn't come across the word*) Tight? Granny was singing
(*Sings*) Ta-r-ra Boom de-ay.
Fred (*No second opinion needed, diagnosis confirmed*)
Pissed.
Narrator The day before the day before yesterday –
now seems more far away
stranger than old Cathay –
– ah, how that tune can stab.
I mix rosemary with a little rue
for the gentlest, most loving soul I ever knew,
my mother's mother.
As I think of her, there floats
down the silent, holy night of memory
a tune which has a gentler poignancy . . .
Carollers While shepherds watched their flocks by night
all seated on the ground . . .
(*The Carol fades*)
Narrator Barefoot I stood on Christmas Day –
my heart gave one great bound –
there, in the firelight, it stood
in gleaming metal, painted wood –
and glory shone around.
Ronald My motor car! Santa's remembered it!
Narrator Cold rapture of the rat-trap pedals bit
and set my bare feet all on fire for joy.
Neville (*He's now two-and-a-threepenny bit*)
Motor car, motor car,
want a ride in motor car!
Ronald It's mine.
(*Motor-mad toad poop-pooppoops*)
Gertie Ronald, Ronald . . .
Jack Hi. Steady on, my boy.
Gertie You're not to be selfish. Neville's your little brother.

Let him get in at once.

Ronald He's got his own toys, Mother.
(*Defiant poops*)

Neville Want motor car. (*Loud wails*)

Narrator The troubles of our proud and angry dust,
eh, Housman? My Shropshire Lad, how right you are.
They came in your time – in my grandchild's time they'll come.
And when I was a boy
to me that glorious toy
was both the pain and joy of martyrdom.
So easy to teach, indeed, so hard to prove
to human hearts, God's joy in brotherly love.
Sisterly love derides man's tongues –
and pen –
for, old or young
to the one cause they stick.
The duchess to her kitchen maid says:

Duchess Men!

Maid They make me sick.

Narrator To which men average, brilliant or dull,
chorus in answer:

Chorus of Men Women are wonderful.

Narrator Mother was wonderful. She used to choke over secret, scented,
gold-tipped cigarettes – it was the dashing thing to do, to smoke,
among the mildly rearguard Suffragettes.
(*Pause, tinkle up teaspoons clatter*)
On second Wednesdays, Mother was At Home.
My hair still feels the hated tug of the comb,
prelude to purgatory:
some twenty minutes (they seemed like hours to me)
being mother's gallant page at afternoon tea.

Ronald (*Most exquisite politeness*) A queen cake, Auntie Muriel? Or an éclair?

Narrator I was blue-eyed, snub-nosed, with Bubbles' curly hair.
Courtesy aunts, whether Missuses or Misses,
were watched like hawks, lest they stooped with loathsome kisses.
Neville rebelled.
(*Infant querulousness*)

The guests departed, he
learned discipline,
(*Hand-smacking, and roars*)
laid over mother's knee.
The treatment – iron hand, no velvet glove – tightened that
strengthening bond of brotherly love.
(*Fade up Neville sobbing*)

Ronald (*All solicitude and fellow-feeling*) Neville, don't cry. I say – I'll let you play
with my soldiers (*hastily*) but not the pack mules...

Neville (*Loud increase of sobs, with fury*) *Go away*!

Narrator My own rebellions were more masked – but yet
held well in check by one, the direct, threat:

Gertie I shall speak to your father.

Narrator A threat more potent than any iron rod.
I loved my father as innocents love God.
(*Reminiscently*) I have his cigarette-case, curved to fit his waistcoat. I've never had the case restored although the corners are battered about a bit from knocking thumb tacks into a drawing-board. In concentrated thought, he used to stick his tongue out at one corner. I have that trick.
(*Fade up a musical comedy tune of mid-1915. Clearly whistled*)
(*More briskly*) But he was whistling, carefree as any ploughboy
one Saturday morning in June,
late June, of 1914, when I was seven...
(*The whistling breaks off*)

Jack Gertie, where's Ronald's sailor hat got to?
Now, boy,
we're off to South Milford
(*Whistle another bar or two. Fade up quiet street background*)
All the world's in tune.
Wave to Mother and Neville.
I'll blow them a kiss.
(*Fingers kissed*)

Ronald (*He is in heaven*) Are we going to see Uncle Harold and Auntie Ciss?

Jack (*To air of Joshua*) Yes, by gosh we are.
(*Off-handed now, knowing effect*) Your uncle's bought a brand-new motor car.

Ronald Oh, Dad, will he take us for a ride in it?

I've longed all my life to ride in a real motor car.
Jack (*Laughing*) What, all your life?
Ronald Every minute of it. Does Uncle Harold drive like mad?
Like Jehu. In the Bible. He drives furiously.
(*Sudden angst*) Are we catching the train at Marsh Lane station?
We'll never catch it. We'll be late, we'll be ever so late!
Jack Shall we? You wait and see.
(*The whistle of a steam train*)
Narrator I paced the platform in jubilant expectation.
(*Whistle nearer*)
Ronald It's coming, it's coming, it's coming, it's coming.
Narrator The snorting green dragon set my child's heart drumming.
(*The train arrives*)
Jack In we get.
(*Carriage door closed. Whistle. Train starts*)
Ronald We're going, we're going! Dad: is South Milford in Lancashire?
Jack It's in Yorkshire.
Ronald But, Dad, listen: the train says
(*Pick up rhythm of wheels*)
To Lancashire, to Lancashire,
to buy a pocket hankashire...
Narrator From rows and rows of houses, the train emerged
through mouths of tunnels
(*Roar, briefly tunnels*)
into green, quiet ways
where fields and woods to the horizon verged,
where horses were startled
(*Horse neigh*)
and cattle at graze.
Ronald Dad, Dad, in one field I've counted twenty-two cows.
(*scornfully*) Dad: Neville calls them moo-cows.
Porter 1 Crossgates.
Porter 2 Garforth.
Porter 3 Micklefield.
Porter 4 South Milford.
(*The train snorts to a stop*)
Jack Here we are.
(*Compartment door opened*)
Ronald (*Disappointed*) Where's Uncle Harold and his motor car?
Jack Going the rounds of his surgeries, I presume;

but he's sent Tom with the gig.

Tom (*About 30, sturdily independent Yorkshireman*)
Good afternoon, Mr Jack.
I'll take the luggage, Doctor's gone to Brotherton.

Jack Tom, you're a jewel.
This is Ronald, my son.

Tom Afternoon, Master Ronald.
(*The pawing of horse hooves on gravel*)
Whoa, Judy! Steady, girl!

Narrator Off we went,
(*Start up spirited dash of horse and gig*)
with a glorious, spinning swirl
of gig wheels and gravel,
past hedges white with June dust
through smells of heat and honeysuckle and just
sniffable undersmells of melted tar,
crossing the closer scent of a cigar.
(*The gig and horse fade*)
The Terrace, when we got there, meant to me:

Ronald Hello, Aunt Ciss.

Narrator Washed hands and (*bored*) afternoon tea.

Ciss (*Practical, no-nonsense doctor's wife*)
Ronald: don't fidget.

Ronald Please, may I go out and play?

Ciss (*Relieved dismissal*) Yes, dear. Of course you may.
(*Fade up garden birds*)

Narrator How vividly my memory re-creates
that afternoon. The Terrace sunned to sleep
over its lawns. The well-raked gravel sweep,
guarded by criss-crossed, timbered, stone-pillared gates.
In my mind's eye I see
on the long lawn a monkey-puzzle tree
with, in its branches, a small, defiant boy
in slashed brown velvet – a Little Lord Fauntleroy.
Like a wild cat he climbed down and came for me,
rolled me upon the grass and overbore me.
I heard my aunt's voice –

Ciss (*Outraged*) Ronald.

Narrator And another –

Mrs. Kemp What, again? (*despair*) Wilfred! Wilfred!

Wilfred (*He is the boy of quick-witted action, a born leader*) Mother.
(*Hiss*) Over the wall, quick. Come on – cut and run

Narrator No time to think, I followed and ran like fun.
(*The running footsteps of two boys, then slowing*)

Wilfred (*Slight panting*) Dodged 'em.
(*He has an attractive voice, if possible with a trace of Irish. Can charm a bird off a bough as well as command it to fly to him*)
I'm Wilfred Kemp. Tell me your name.

Ronald Ronald Scriven.

Wilfred (*Self-defence*) Mother made me wear this beastly suit
because it's my birthday.
(*Honour satisfied by alibi*)
Come on, let's play a game.
I know. Detectives! I'll be Sexton Blake
and you can be Drerr Dread.

Ronald Drerr Dread?

Wilfred Yes, yes. Doctor Dread, you coot!
He's the villain I'm going to catch, alive or dead.
He goes about baring his teeth – ss, ss, like this,.

Ronald I think I ought to go back. Auntie Ciss...

Wilfred (*High scorn*) You're not a cissie, are you?

Ronald No, I'm not!

Wilfred Prove it. You've got a bloodstained knife in a shoulder-sheath.
But nobody ever gives Sexton Blake the slip
and I paralyse you in an iron grip
when I and Tinker unmask your fiendish plot –
then you're at bay, see? And mind you bare your teeth.

Ronald (*Committed, but cautious*) Can I be Tinker? We could have a pretend Drerr Dread.

Wilfred (*Very firmly*) No we couldn't.
(*Magnanimously*) But you can have as many pretend villains as you like,
dozens of 'em, for me and Tinker to strike
(*Thrillingly*) at midnight, in your sepulchral vault, stone dead.

Narrator Long before midnight, tired, fearful, hot,
I parted from Wilfred.

Wilfred Come on! Over the wall!
(*Scrabblings over wall*)
I say, that's funny. Your sailor top's got wet.
Just sneak in like Deerfoot the Deerslayer – and don't forget

our secret blood brother sign – the Grey Owl call.
(*Instant piercing double hoot, awfully bad imitation*)

Narrator The grapes of my aunt's wrath were diluted by my tears.

Ciss I shall speak to your father as soon as he comes in.

Narrator Father and Uncle Harold connived at sin.

Harold (*Rather dry*) Weathered the storm yet, Admiral?
(*The professional quick eye*)
Let's have a look at that thumb.
Broken glass? No . . .

Jack It's a nasty cut.

Harold Come, come,
kids playing with blunt knives, Jack. I'll dress the wound.

Narrator The antiseptic bit. At the sight of blood
I nearly swooned.
But his surgeon's hands seemed as though they understood
my very flesh.

Harold You didn't wince much. Good.

Ronald Uncle, can Wilfred come for a ride with us tomorrow –
in your motor car? After church, of course, I mean.

Harold (*A wise man*) We'll see what your aunt says.

Narrator My aunt refused. And sorrow's cup of sorrow was full
on Monday, when all the world was June gold-green
and I was still in my Aunt Ciss's blackest books.
(*The quiet ticking of a clock, and listless knife-and-fork*)

Ciss Ronald: don't toy with your breakfast.

Ronald No, Aunt Ciss.
(*Horrible owl hoots from Wilfred outside*)

Narrator I sat up with a jerk.

Ronald Please may I leave . . .

Ciss (*Irritated*) You may not. You're not going out
until I take you to the Middlebrooks this afternoon.

Ronald But Wilfred . . .

Narrator No use at all to pout.
After lunch, she marched me along
beside a stream
(*Water-gurgles*)
which sang to itself in the afternoon's long dream
with silence and birdsong blent.
(*Blend them, with brook undertones*)
We came to a garden, where

a willow wept, like a fountainous green tent.
(Birds and stream out but swallows in)

Ciss Here we are.
(The click of a garden gate opening.)
There's Mrs Middlebrook, over there.

Mrs Middlebrook *(Calling)* Good afternoon.

Ciss And her two little daughters.

Narrator *(Gloomily)* That was splendid news.

Ciss *(Very cordial)* Good afternoon.
(Hiss) Ronald: mind your p's and q's.

Mrs Middlebrook So this is Ronald. Well dear, this is Claire.

Claire *(Shyly)* Hello.

Ronald *(Unwilling politeness)* How do you do?

Peggy *(Much more confident)* Hello. I'm Peggy.
(A growl, quiet, menacing)
Trigger, shut up. Mother, may we take Ronald to play?

Mrs Middlebrook Of course you may.

Narrator A sturdy little girl, too short to be leggy,
she grabbed my hand. Claire shyly took the other,
and off we went.
(Fade up a stream and wagtails)
The banks of the stream were afroth
with daisies. High in the sky the swallows swooped.
Over the stream the hazels, full-leaved, drooped
and water-wagtails murmured brief refrains.

Peggy Oh, I do love being by the beck.
I know, I know: we'll both make daisy chains
to hang round Ronald's neck.

Narrator I sat beside them on the grass, distraught.
Rather than daisy chains, the fire, the rack.
Suppose that Wilfred saw me? At the thought
the sun turned black.
Trigger, the gun-dog, glad to be alive
startled the wagtails with a belly-dive.
(Loud water-splash)

Peggy Trigger! He only dives in the beck to shake the water all over us.

Claire He would.
(Water surge)

Peggy Look what he's got
in his mouth.

Ronald (*Excited, relief from boredom*) A whopping big jam-pot.
There's something wriggling out of it. A snake, a snake!
Peggy Don't be silly, an eel. Oh, quick, quick, Ronald: catch it.
(*Trigger barks*)
Narrator While Trigger barked about, I tried to snatch it.
Ronald (*Astonished*) It's slippery.
Peggy Of course it is, you sap.
Claire (*Shrill apprehension*) Mind – it'll bite you.
Peggy (*Practical girl*) Grab it with your cap.
Ronald Got it!
Peggy Let's put it in the water butt by our granary stairs
and fish for it with a bent pin.
Narrator The wobbling Cyclops eye of the sun
smithereened as one by one
we fished for that eel, turn about,
until Claire heard her mother shout:
Mrs Middlebrook (*Distant*)
Tea, children.
Narrator Transparent jellies, ruby-bright,
home-bottled pears a-billow
with yellow cream, thick soda scones to bite
beside the weeping willow.
Was ever garnered fruit without a speck?
Claire, shy Claire, clasped her arms around my neck:
Claire Ronald's my sweetheart.
Narrator Earth refused to swallow
my scarlet shame.
As Omar looked, I looked at the sky's blue hollow
and as the Perisian got, I got the same
blank, dusty answer. And like Drerr Dread
I bared my teeth.
Ciss Has the child been stung by a wasp?
Narrator My good aunt said.
Afterwards, in the lane, she touched my curls
Ciss (*Brisk approval, no trace of sentiment*)
I'm glad you got on with those nice little Middlebrook girls.
(*Fades background*)
Narrator In the dusk the magic casement curtains stirred.
(*A distant slow goods train toots*)
A sleepy goods train answered a hunting owl.

Ronald (*Intense misery*) I'm *not* Claire's sweetheart.
Narrator Suppose that Wilfred heard?
Deerslayer's braves were always on the prowl.
I heard their stealthy footsteps in the woods
giving the call sign
(*The hoot, twice, of a genuine owl*)
answered by the goods.
(*Sleepier, more distant chuffs of the train fading*)
Next morning
all my world seemed dark as Dis.
(*The quiet ticking of the clock and listless knife and fork*)
Ciss Don't toy with your breakfast, child.
Ronald No Auntie Ciss.
(*Sharply, Wilfred's owl-hoot*)
Wilfred!
(*Under breath*) He's found out.
Narrator Then answer to prayer, from
my aunt herself –
Ciss Why not go to the stables with Tom?
Narrator I trotted along the Terrace by Tom's side
to keep pace with his stride.
(*A bulldog snores*)
By the harness room a bulldog of brindled colour
with a spiked collar, snored in the sun.
Tom That's Buller.
(*Caressingly*) Eh, you old fool.
(*Flat voice*) Doctor's dog. Bought him at medical school.
Your auntie says he smells, so now he's mine.
That's his motor car in the coach-house.
(*Contemptuously*) A Sunbeam.
I've got to mend it. 'Tisn't in my line.
Motor cars! Attend to an 'oss's needs
and it won't break down and leave you in the soup.
(*Wilfred's owl-call*)
Narrator Wilfred. He was on me with a whoop.
Wilfred Didn't you hear our secret Indian call?
Tom I reckon half South Milford did, an' all.
Wilfred Come on. Through the orchard. Climb the paddock gate.
Narrator The paddock was like a rough pony, with a patch –
the tennis court – clipped neatly from its coat,

as green as green, with a summerhouse to match
except that its paint was sun-blistered.

Wilfred The giant's castle. Follow me. Swim the moat,
scale the walls and storm the castle keep.

Narrator Inside the summerhouse, summer lay asleep.
We opened a square window of frosted glass,
and saw milk-maided, bee-orchised, buttercupped grass
grazed by a white horse.

Wilfred Good old Snowball.

Narrator Fond memory recalls
the sultry heat between those wooden walls,
and a chest crammed with hoops, mallets and croquet balls.

(*A heavy lid is lifted*)

Wilfred Cannon balls. I'm Admiral Lord Nelson. You
are my captain, Hardy. Take your orders from me.
'That's easy, Hardy. All you've got to do
is just to steer my flagship, Victory.
Death to the French. Look, Hardy, the water runs with blood.'

Ronald The cannon-mouths are all red-hot.

Wilfred Another broadside from the starboard guns.

(*Wooden echoes from dropped croquet balls. Crack of mallet handle.*)

(*noticeably coolly*) Hardy: I think I'm shot.

(*A light thud as he falls*)

Ronald The French are hauling down their colours.

Wilfred Good.
I'm dying. Kiss, me, Hardy.

Ronald Mother said
he really meant 'Kismet'.

Wilfred 'Course he didn't, you dunce.
Everyone knows his last words.
Kiss me at once.

(*A reluctant kiss*)

Now make my death mask.
I'll tell you when I'm dead.
Lash me in canvas, weighted with cannon balls
and loads and loads of grapeshot and round shot.
(*Hastily*) No. I forgot.
Pickle my body in a brandy cask.
Hardy, my last command. Now do your duty

and sail me back to England, home and beauty.
Give me a hero's funeral. You're in charge.
Row me past Greenwich in my Admiral's Barge
with black oars and my coffin under a black awning.
All London will line the banks and the Tower walls.
Simply everybody will be simply *plastered* in mourning.
(*Rapturously*) Hardy, bury me in my glory in St Paul's.

Narrator A solemn moment of history. We sang –

Both Rule, Britannia, Britannia, rule the waves,
Britons . . .
(*Loud, sudden shotgun, both barrels*)

Narrator So close to hand was the double, startling bang
that Snowball shied.

Wilfred (*Carelessly, he's a country boy*) Somebody taking a pot-shot.

Narrator The countryside
soon settled its green dove-wings in the heat.
But faraway, in a Sarajevo street,
a sharper gun-shot rang –
(*Very distant pistol shot*)
Its echo in London was readily translated
and yelled by newsboys above the Fleet Street thunder –
(*Fade up 1914 traffic*)

Newsboy (*Slight Cockney*) Speshul! Austrian Archduke assassinated.

Narrator (*Ironically*) A nine hours wonder.
(*Fade traffic*)
Rupert of Hentzau was far better known
in stay-at-home England than the out-of-favour heir
to Austro-Hungary's imperial throne.
This was none of our affair.
The name of Sarajevo meant as little
to all save a stray of travellers, a dryness of dons,
and an eccentricity of other cattle, as little
as the name of Mons.
When the news was shouted in London streets that day
who guessed from so small a cloud in the central blue
that war was a garden-party month away?

Grey We shall not sheathe the sword, which we have not lightly drawn.

Voice It'll be over by Christmas

Voice (*Complete faith*) The Navy . . .

Voice (*Matching faith*) The Army . . .

Voice Who does Kaiser Bill think he is?
Voice He's barmy.
Narrator That was the mood on the eve of Armageddon.
War was an extra excitement small boys fed on
as a change from cowboys and Indians, Sexton Blake.
War was glorious – and vague –
a game we played for imagination's sake.
We had fought the Sioux. We beat the Prussian Guards.
I was Sir John French to Wilfred's Douglas Haig.
We learned our armoury from cigarette cards.
Wilfred Swap a field ambulance for an M.T.B.?
Ronald Not a fair swap. You know I've only one.
Wilfred (*Charming a bird off a bush*) I want it to complete my set, Ron. See –
the Royal Horse Artillery's cap badge. Done?
Ronald (*With resignation*) Done.
Narrator Golden days in South Milford, in the sun
which shone forever on the meadowsweet
when I was there with Wilfred, and we roamed
meadows and pastures, woods, the High Street and the Low Street,
until, like homing pigeons, tired we homed
at evening, to alight
and sleep, contented, beneath the wing of night.
(*The distant sleepy train's pleasant steam whistle*)
Roused by the whistled warning
of the Slow Selby Milk
I saw the lawns of morning,
dew-shimmering like shot-silk.
Wilfred (*'Orrible owl-call*) Come out the instant second breakfast's over.
I've invented an invention – in our back yard.
Narrator He was sucking Nectar from a head of clover
and had the air of Arnold Bennett's Card.
Wilfred The most wonderful invention ever known:
Look, Ron – The Wilfred Kemp Field Telephone!
Narrator It had superb simplicity of design:
a couple of holed empty cocoa tins
connected by several yards of brisket twine.
The proud inventor looked at it, with pins
and needles of excitement in his eyes.
He gave me my orders:

Wilfred There are German spies
all round us. This telephone is the only link
with our artillery. Now then, let me think.
We'll run the line from the observation post –
your bathroom window – to me, in command of the guns
and then we'll have the enemy on toast.
Death to the Huns.

Narrator I was shouting information when I heard:

Ciss Ronald...

Ronald Hold on a minute, Wilfred.
Yes, Auntie Ciss.

Ciss Some good news for you, Ronald. I've just heard
from your mother.

Narrator She gave me an unexpected kiss.

Ciss You've got a baby sister. Isn't that splendid?

(*Fade up the slow start of a steam train*)

Narrator The train departed dead on Bradshaw time.
Late summer and early autumn were so blended,
the swallows seemed reluctant to depart.
The leaves were darker – even the leaves of the lime.
As the smells of all green things blend after rain,
field merged with wood and wood with country lane.
Down the perspective of half a century
I see, I see
that landscape, caught by an artist's brush, suspended
for one brief hour – and eternity.
Somewhere between South Milford and Leeds, long ago
the train ran out of that landscape and was lost.
Was it at Micklefield? Was it at Barnbow?
No, no. The point's impossible to trace.
The line is marked in time, but not in space,
an invisible intangible boundary I crossed
where the kingdom of boyhood, I shared with Wilfred, ended.

(*The train stops at the terminus*)

Granny met me, stooping to imprint
kisses of White Heather, and love, and peppermint.

Grandmother My, how you've grown! Let's have a look at you.

Ronald How's Mother, Granny?
Granny, I've got a friend.
His name is Wilfred Kemp. I like him no end.

He can climb the tallest tree you ever knew.
Wilfred could climb a church tower if he wanted to.
Wilfred . . .
(*Cross-fade the terminus with an old cab horse*)

Narrator I rattled on
like a cab, with a horse fit only for the knacker.

Grandmother Poor thing. The war. All the other horses have gone.
(*The cab stops*)

Narrator Neville rushed out like a jumping Chinese cracker:

Neville Ron, I've got a drum.
Ron, I've got a bugle. Ron,
come and play with me. I've got lots of soldiers too.

Ronald (*Instant suspicion*) If you've broken my gun mules . . .

Neville (*Begins guilty whisper*) Daddy mended . . .

Ronald You little blister!

Grandmother That will do.
He's been so looking forward to seeing you today.
Go and play with him while I put my things away.
Then I'll take you to see your baby sister.

Ronald Don't want to see her. It's Mother I want to see.

Neville And me. Take me.

Grandmother (*Some hesitation, important information being withheld*)
Not just now, dear.

Ronald But Auntie Cissie said
Mother wanted . . .

Grandmother (*Obvious evasion*) But of course, by and by.
In a day or two – perhaps.

Narrator How startlingly the bird of instinct flaps
at children and other small wings of warning.

Ronald I want to see Mother! Why can't I see her? Why?

Grandmother We mustn't disturb her, darling . . . Mother's in bed.

Ronald When will Dad come home from the works?

Grandmother Not till ever so late.
But I'll sit up and wait
(*Soothing syrup ladled out*) And maybe you'll see Mother in the morning.

Narrator In the morning Father came in to us, sad and gay:

Jack Well, now.
You're not too big
for a come-home kiss?

Ronald Daddy . . . oh, Daddy!

Jack How's Uncle Harold? Aunt Ciss?
I'm working up to eighteen hours a day.
Oh Lord, for one long weekend at South Milford.

Ronald Why can't I see Mother, Dad?
Granny can see her.

Neville And Anna.

Ronald And baby Ruth.

Jack Mother's not very well. She won't even see me, my lad.
Soon, when she's better, perhaps a week or two.
Now I must dash. Be good boys, both of you.

Narrator His eyes smiled, out of rims of tiredness.
He turned at the door:

Jack Good morning – and God bless.

Neville But why can Anna see her?

Ronald And Granny?

Neville *And* baby Ruth?

Narrator So we went and asked Anna.
She made her fingers snap:

Anna (*Overworked, bothered*) Out of my kitchen.

Neville No use!

Ronald Not a scrap!

Narrator It was Fred, the paper-boy, who told me the truth.
He whistled me through the letter-box flap.
(*Whistle*)

Fred (*Through letter-box*) I'll gie ye three comics if ye'll gie us a cig.
Good 'uns. The Rainbow. Comic Cuts. And Chips.

Ronald I haven't got one.

Fred Yer Ma has. With gold tips.
She's had all her teeth out. Gow, she bled like a pig.
Go on, pinch a packet.

Ronald (*Angry and upset*) I won't.

Narrator I sat on the staircase and felt sick.

Neville Play with me.

Ronald Go away! (*More gently*)
Talk to Anna. I don't want to play.

Narrator I stared at familiar things I understood:
mirror, hatstand, umbrella, walking stick.
Imagination mouthed at me:

Imagination (*Dreadful voice, soft*) Blood . . . blood . . . blood . . .

her mouth is full of blood.
(*A cold wind is heard*)

Narrator I tried the front door, standing tiptoe on the mat.
(*Rattle of door handle*)
It was locked.

Grandmother (*Upstairs*) Ronald: you've not to go out. I've told you that.

Narrator I pushed up the metal flap of the letter-box
which was level with my eyes.
(*Letter-box flap lifted. Cold wind louder*)
Near the garden gate the steepling hollyhocks
rocked in the wind. I heard the cries
of errand boys, the ping of bicycle bells.
With swinging crutches, two men in hospital blue
limped along on the other side of the avenue.
I was gripped by the fascination which compels
the secret watcher to observe, spellfast.
(*Horses and a gun-carriage go by*)
A field artillery battery trotted past.
The kaleidoscopic scene absorbed, engrossed
my boy's mind. I forgot about my mother,
and heedless of draughts, as of my little brother,
day after day manned my observation-post.
So long as I was quiet, nobody cared
what I was doing. Why should they? I stared
at the great world, until at last
one morning my grandmother said:

Grandmother (*Ordinary I-want-you voice*) Ronald.

Narrator I turned my head,
and heard her cry aghast
at the sight of my streaming face.

Grandmother Oh, *RONALD*!

Narrator My nostrils were blocked by phlegm,
my eyes were inflamed and gummed by mucous glue.

Grandmother *RONALD*!

Narrator She laid me on the settee and tried to dry
the rolling tears.

Ronald Don't, Granny – my eyes are smarting.

Narrator A nerve throbbed at the corner of my eye.

Grandmother (*Great concern*) Your eyes are bloodshot.

Narrator The sound of her voice, I heard,

but indistinctly, as though a train were departing.,
carrying me away. The colours of things were blurred,
ceiling and walls seemed paler or deeper red.
The nerve throbbed again. There were voices in my head:

Pain (*Very cold*) Listen to me. My name is Pain.
I've touched you, lightly, before.
Now I'm going to hurt you
(*Ronald cries out sharply*)
and again . . . and again . . . and again.
Here . . . and here.
I shall drive a red-hot screw into each ear.
I am patient. I am slow and I am merciless.
(*Now he's really moaning. Other voices are blurred and muffled – coming and going*)

Grandmother Anna, Anna, quick!
Bring me a hot boiled onion in a woollen sock.

Narrator I put my hands to my ears and tried to press the ache away.

Anna (*Faint, but audible*) The onion, ma'am. Poor lamb, poor lamb!

Ronald (*Shouts*) Don't, don't! It burns my ear.

Anna Poor little lamb.

Narrator (*His voice is clear and has remembered anguish, not self-pity*) Heat and the turn of the screw seemed to interlock
touch, sight and sound into one crimson sense.
Time ebbed . . . flowed back, and pain was less intense:
I heard one sound, shrill in the treble clef.

Neville (*Weeping*) Don't cry, Ron.

Ronald Daddy!

Grandmother He's coming.

Ronald (*Shouts*) I can't hear what you say. Mother! Mother!

Narrator Voices, voices . . . fading away.
I had entered another kingdom, that of the deaf.
(*Long pause*)

Doctor Osteitis media. He will never hear
again in his left ear.
Later . . perhaps . . he might
regain some minimal hearing in his right.
(*Long pause*)

Narrator (*Philosophical, quite light-hearted*)
All early in the April
my small world was dew-bright

and full of sound and colour
and quick with birds in flight.

Cuckoo Cuckoo.

Narrator I learned, through my five senses,
direct but subtle things:
the lovely like-unlike between
the green of wheat and barley-green,
the slightly varied, different beat
of thrush and blackbird wings.
The tang of Ribston Pippin,
the Bramley Seedling's bite.
The touch of elm-bark and dry wall,
the smell of morning's primroses
and noonday's cowslip ball:
all early in the April
I learned and loved them all.

Cuckoo (*Very early call*) Cuckoo.

Narrator I have dwelled in the wasteland's oases
for a brief hour or so.
Have I seen a mirage in the desert?
Is the wasteland the illusion? I do not know.
I know only that I must journey on
towards the approaching snow.
Heart, feel no pang.
An English poet, after a Roman sang:
'Still are thy pleasant voices,
Thy nightingales awake;
for Death, he taketh all away
but them he cannot take.'
Heart, do not ache.
Loved voices in your head still say: –

Grandmother (*A little tipsily*) Oranges. Tarara BOOM de ay!

Gertie With the flat of my hairbrush now he's three
I teach him manners across my knee.

Narrator (*Laughing*) Ah, even so, even so.

Jack (*Singing*) Ten, twenty, thirty, forty,
fifty years ago.

The Peacock Screamed One Morning

The Peacock Screamed One Morning was first broadcast on BBC Radio 4 on 25 March 1970 with the following cast:

NARRATOR	*Stephen Murray*
RONALD SCRIVEN	*Judy Bennett*
NEVILLE SCRIVEN	*Jo Manning Wilson*
SLOW JOE ROBINSON	*David March*
IRON ANN	*Kathleen Helme*
UNCLE JAMES	*Frederick Treves*
EDGAR	*Elizabeth Proud*
EDITH SWAINE	*Hilda Schroder*

Produced by Charles Lefeaux

(*Fade up Music – Pavane Op. 20 by Fauré*)
which is stopped by the single scream of a peacock)

Narrator Look at the sky
embossed with worlds, stars, suns, and damascened
with shimmering Milky Ways:
it is God's shield,
protecting mortal sight
from the unendurable light
men call eternity.
(*Fade up spring birds*)
Long ago, as we reckon the count of our days
my boyhood's innocence screened
my eyes from this knowledge. I lay in an English field
under the shadow of Wearybones Hill and gazed
at the spring clouds drifting by.
Between the sun and the field, with a scarce-perceptible glide
from side to side,
a kestrel, wind-hovering, eyed
with a glance of brilliant glass
each tuft of grass
which a field-mouse might stir against the wind's breath
and ... so ... attract the instant swoop of death.
What did death mean to me? I was aware
of his name, as vaguely as, down the cool spring air
I sensed the kestrel's floating shadow pass.
I looked at the sky and knew that God was there.
God, Who – the thought came drifting into my head –
loved Mrs Radcliffe – so, Aunt Ciss had said,
God wanted her in heaven. Now she was dead.
We'd been very impressed, I and Neville, my younger brother.

Ronald Mrs Radcliffe's an angel now, Neville, with wings and a golden harp.
Perhaps God loved her for being Uncle Harold's mother.

Neville (*He is about four-and-fourpence to my ninepence plus a bit*)
Does she wear a white nightie, too?

Narrator Against the blue
bridging the sky between the whaleback scarp
of Wearybones and North Rigton Hill, I tried

to picture Angel Mrs Radcliffe, winging
her way above the Glassy Sea and singing
Hymns A. and M., her voice a little flat,
as it was when she went to South Milford church, adorning
the fourth pew from the front, of a Sunday morning,
in lavender Ottoman silk and a flowered hat.
So sharp was her image on my inward eye,
her dead voice in my inward ear
so clear,
that imagination had but to pierce the sky
to see and hear,
among the cherubim,
chanting my favourite hymn –

Mrs Radcliffe (*Sings to harp*) All thing bright and beautiful,
all creatures great and small . . .

Ronald (*In a self-hypnotising chant*) Angel Mrs Radcliffe, Angel
Mrs Radcliffe . . .

Narrator From the tail of my eye I saw the kestrel close
his wings and plunge, like a red-brown falling star,
and brake his speed to strike as the field-mouse froze
too late. I did not hear
its thin, high shriek. Such sounds no longer passed
the obstinate barrier of my middle ear
which deafness some ten months before had sealed.
Up I sprang, as the kestrel rose and flew
with wing-beats fast
towards his nest in the tallest tree of three
in the far corner of the eighty-acre field.

Ronald Whoo-whoop.

Narrator I made the secret Indian call
which Wilfred Kemp, my hero, and I had whooped
in my beloved South Milford. Off I went,
running, as a fox runs, in the shadow of the hedge,
not over the open field. I was intent
on robbery. I knew Joe, Slow Joe,
Joe Robinson, the husband of Iron Ann
of Low Moor Farm, into whose hands my brother
and I had fallen, was lurking somewhere or other –
and robbing the kestrel's nest was a thing forbidden.
Even so,

I began to climb, as Wilfred had taught me to.
The oak was not in full leaf. I was not hidden
as much as I thought I was. Half-way up ...

Joe (*Deep voice, very Yorkshire*)
Halloooo.
(*Bark of cattle dog, collie type*)
Get out o' that tree.

Narrator From a limb of the oak I could see
Slow Joe, broad as a beer barrel, grey cloth-capped,
with a black, Newgate fringe of an ill-clipped beard
stalking across the big field, the Rasser, in a paddy,
followed, as always, by his shadow, Laddie,
his black-and-white cattle dog. Fear began to melt
my bones within me. My racing heart nearly stopped
and as I dropped
the last few feet, I saw his hands, with deliberation, go
to the buckle of his belt.

Joe I'll learn thee.
(*Swishing of belt, hard punishment, slow and thorough*)

Ronald Don't ... don't ... oh, don't.
(*Heavy sobs*)

Joe Happen, next time, you'll think on what I tell't you.
Kestrels is t' farmer's friends.

Narrator In memory's nostril blends
the light East wind keenness of the Rasser's air, the cleanness
of earth and grass and new leaves,
and the farmyard, byre, pigsty and sheepfold smell
of Slow Joe's clothes –
the full smell of the land.
I see Windhoverer wheel –
ah, and I feel
the tongue of Laddie, licking salt from the back of my tear-wet hand.

Joe (*Matter-of-fact, lesson having been taught*)
Missus wants you. Look sharp.

Narrator He turned on his heel.
Laddie, like a shadow dragged against the sun,
followed his master. I began to run.
I neared the grim, stone house
which the April sunlight seemed to make more grey.

The straggly garden, in front of the farm, abutted
on an oval of grass, where daises lay like hail.
There, jewelled, lordly among his pea-hens, strutted
Pharaoh, Iron Ann's peacock, with fan-spread tail.
(*The peacock screams*)
I stood and watched him advance, retreat, advance
to tread the measure of his courtship dance.
Dazzled, fascinated by the wondrous fan
I did not hear the voice of Iron Ann...

Ann (*About 60, rather a light, markedly Yorkshire voice, imperious*)
Ronald.
(*Pause*)

Narrator Her fingers, bony, hard as those of a man,
gripped the lobe of my ear.

Ann (*Note: she uses the word 'naughty' in its Elizabethan sense, connoting wickedness – as the Elizabethan's called deadly nightshade Naughty Man's Cherries, meaning the Devil's*)
Yeou naughty boy. You're as black as t' chimney back.
Into the scullery, off with your shirt. I'll scrub ye.
Your Uncle James is here.

Narrator With hard pump-water and harder yellow soap
I scrubbed myself. Ann's scrutinising eye
regarded me as through a microscope.

Ann Wash t'back of yer knees again.

Narrator As clean and dry
as the scrubbed flagstones of Ann's kitchen floor
I stood on the rag rug in front of the fire. The kettle
jetted thin steam and there, laid out on the settle...

Ronald My clothes! The clothes I used to wear at home..
My sailor top!

Narrator At home. How I had hated
those second Wednesdays when, 'At Home' my mother
had combed my curls and dressed
my baby brother
to be cooed at and admired
by courtesy aunts who called us 'little dears'.
I looked – and into my eyes welled a desolation of tears.

Ann (*Sharply*) What's up wi' thee?

Ronald It's my clothes. I want to go home, I want to go home.

Ann (*Irritably rather than harshly: she has no imagination*)
Yeou know varry well you can't. There's nobody there.
Thi mother's in hospital.
Thi father an' all
– and like to be
this many a month. Crying? A big lad like thee?
Neville's nobbut a bairn.

Ronald But why do we have to stay here?

Ann Because thi Uncle says so.
Now get thissen dressed. He's in't parlour wi' thi brother.
Tha'll have thi teas in theer.

Narrator My feet, after clogs, felt strange in my own shoes.
The passage smelt of cleanliness next to godliness.
(*Light boy's footsteps echoing on stone*)
The parlour –
(*Creak of an opened door. Tick of a grandfather clock*)
smelled of godliness itself.
Mirrors of the triple-mirrored mantelshelf
reflected, not God, but someone scarcely less
omnipotent in my eyes. Yes: Uncle James was there.
He sat, knees apart, in a black-prickly, horsehair-stuffed armchair.
All six foot odd and nineteen stone of him.

James How are you, Ronald my boy?

Ronald Very well, thank you, Uncle James.

James So you look. I'm sure you two enjoy
life on a farm, good food, fresh country air.
No doubt Mrs Robinson looks after you and your brother
– good, homely body – as though she were your mother.
And, I may add,
this life'll make a man of you, my lad.

Ronald (*Complete lack of conviction*) Yes, Uncle.
(*Eagerly*) How's Dad?

James (*Guardedly*) Oh . . . as well as can be expected, Ronald.
No better . . . but I'm glad to say, no worse.
These things take time.

Ronald Yes, Uncle. How's Mother?

James Up and down, Ronald. No doubt she'll write you a letter
when she feels well enough.

Ronald (*Vehemently*) Why can't I see them?

Neville I'd kiss Mummy better.

James (*Somewhat testily*) Hospital rules.

Narrator Childless, he was shy with children, often terse.

(*A knock on the door*)

Ann (*Utterly different tone with James, not the least servile, but very civil*)
Happen you'd like your tea now, Mr James?

James (*Changed tone, relieved*) By all means. I can see the table's laid,
and the smell from the kitchen certainly proclaims
good things to come.

Ann I'se done me best. Ham's home-cured, eggs is fresh.

James Eh, capital. And all the rest home-made?

Narrator My uncle, a redoubtable trencherman,
beamed on the ham and eggs and beamed at Ann.

James Ah, a dish from a lost world. Farmhouse ham-and-eggs
such as I used to relish on walking tours
in the old days, when England was at peace.
Precious few of us, I can tell you, get food like this
in nineteen-seventeen.
No wonder you look like two young fighting cocks.

Ronald Uncle...

Narrator I wanted to tell him how, at breakfast-time
on my first morning under Iron Ann's roof,
she gave me oatmeal porridge, in a bowl
aswim with skimmed milk, to revolt the soul,
and bobbing with podge-lumps hard as a horse's hoof.

Ronald (*Politely*) I don't want this porridge, thank you Mrs Robinson.

Ann It's none what tha wants, it's what tha's getting.

Ronald But Mrs Robinson, I can't eat it, really I *can't*.

Ann Aye? Tha'll get nowt else till tha diz then, that tha shan't.
When tha wants it – ask for it.

Narrator She looked at me over her steel-framed glasses, then, setting
the loathsome bowl on the mantelshelf out of my reach,
went into the dairy. Slow Joe, sparse of speech
(he seldom uttered a word in the house) guffawed.

Joe (*Guffaw*) Oatmeal builds your strength up. Look at me.

(*He does one or two gorilla chest-thumps*)

Narrator I had three days of no breakfast, no dinner, no tea
and supperless to bed. When hunger gnawed
I tried to hold it with pride's curbing bit.

Ann gave me the porridge at once when I asked for it.
(*The clock ticks*)
Now I looked at my uncle and words I wanted to say
stuck in my throat, like those podge-lumps grizzly-grey.
He'd not understand. 'Course not. He'd be on Ann's side.
Had I been older, I might have glimpsed, lurking, shy,
in the suspicious tail of his bright blue eye
the jolly fat uncle, who wore a cracker crown
at children's parties in the Masonic Hall
and had a pocketful of sweets, not posies
(*Cross-fade clock to piano – Ring-a-ring-a-roses*)
where little girls shrieked

Tots Ring-a-ring-a-roses

Narrator sneezed –

James (*With it*) 'Tishoo, TISHOO
ALL fall down.
(*Fall them down, mixing shrieks of party into Neville's whoop of delight and clock tick*)

Narrator I looked at Neville, scandalised to see
the little traitor sitting, ride-a-cock horse,
on Uncles James's knee.

James Rings on her fingers and bells on her toes –

Neville (*Shouting at top of voice*) – she shall have music wherever she goes.

Narrator Outside the window, which looked on Wearybones Hill,
Pharaoh, Ann's peacock, slept on a dry wall,
with his folded train draped, like a witch's shawl
she'd cast aside, having worked her wicked will.

Ronald (*Under breath, but clearly audible*)
The witch's parlour window has been nailed down.
The nails and the wood
have been painted in a horrible sort of brown.
(*A little louder, with inspired conviction*)
I know. The witch mixed the paint with her victim's blood.

James What did you say?

Ronald Nothing, Uncle. Uncle, may I play
on Mrs Robinson's piano, please?

James I don't suppose she'll mind.

Narrator Each of the yellow keys
was as clean as the tooth of a hound
nor did my dulled ear detect one faulty sound.

(*In strict time on old, not too badly tuned piano, tune only:*)

Ronald 'Oh, I can wash my father's shirt,
Oh, I can wash it clean,
Oh, I can wash my father's . . .'

Neville (*With a rush, banging three keys with fist*)
I want to play, let *me* play.
(*Another random bang*)

Narrator I tried to pull my little brother away.

Neville Let *me*, let *me*!

Narrator I pushed him.
(*Light thud, brief howl of astonishment, not hurt*)
Over he went.
Despair, grief, wretchedness and anger, pent
within my being, burst out ferociously.
I sobbed. I hammered the keyboard with both fists.
(*Fists on piano con furioso ma non virtuoso*)

James (*Through 'music' as though getting through to hysterical boy*)
. . . to your senses . . . this nonsense . . . at once, Ronald . . .
Do you hear me? . . . Stop
(*Piano thumping stops*)

Ronald (*All passion spent*) Yes, Uncle.

Narrator He was holding both my wrists,
I tried to pull my hands back.
I felt as though all my innards had gone slack.

James Now tell your brother you're sorry.

Ronald I'm sorry, Neville.

Narrator His lower lip trembled and he wouldn't come near me.
My trish-trash polka piano-tantrum drew
no thunder-and-lightning cloudburst from Iron Ann
when she reappeared. Her faded eyes, ice-blue,
had, stamped at each corner, a crinkly crow's foot fan
as she stood at her door to bid my uncle adieu.

James Well, Mrs Robinson, I'm satisfied altogether
with the way you're looking after these two boys.
A great relief to . . .
(*A single scream from the peacock*)
What on earth was that noise?

Ann (*Cackle of laughter*) My peacock, Pharaoh, knows a change in t'weather
afore it happens.

James (*Surprised*) Why, he's up there on the barn.

Ann Aye: he flew.

James He has a magnificent tail.
You must be proud of him, Mrs Robinson.

Ann (*Very complacently, but reined in*) Nay –
not a farmer's wife can boast the like in't t'dale.

Narrator Neville rode on his uncle's shoulder all the way
past the home meadow, where the old snow-plough lay,
past the twelve-acre, spear-pointed with winter wheat,
its columns of furrows marching up to the railway line.
(*Lapwings in spring are heard*)
Lapwings tumbled about as they had drunk new wine.

James Down you get. Here's the level-crossing gate.
(*Klok of signal arm dropping. A distant slow passenger train is approaching*)
Never cross when the signal's down, Ronald. Always wait.

Ronald But it's safe now, Uncle.

James You're deaf. You can't hear the train.

Neville I can!

Narrator I climbed on the gate and in a little while
a dragon in faded colours of green and gold
majestically rolled
its smoked-wreathed body over the crossing in style –
and even my ears heard the gay refrain:

Soldiers (*Passing in train*) Pack up your troubles in your old kit-bag
and smile, smile, smile.

James Did you notice the red-cross markings, Ronald?
War wounded – poor devils –
(*Train and chorus fading in distance*)
Well: I'll say goodbye. Be good boys.
Your Aunt Flo sends her love and a big kiss
for each of you . . .

Narrator He brushed up his moustache.
(*Two kisses*)

Ronald Uncle: can I have my toys?
My Meccano, my gun mules and my fort and my pedal motor car,
oh, all my toys, please, Uncle . . .
(*Patent afterthought*) . . . and, of course, Neville's.

James (*Slight surprise*) What's this?

I sent them to Low Moor weeks ago, weeks ago.
Well, wartime!
If you don't get them soon, let me know.

Narrator He crossed our palms with silver – a fortune each.

James Goodbye. God Bless.

Narrator I waved, struck dumb of speech.
Then, taking Neville's hand, I turned away.

Neville Our toys are coming. Hurray, hurray, hurray!
Ron, can I have a ride in your motor car
as soon as it comes?
(*Outburst of generosity*) You can play with my teddy-bear.

Ronald We're not going to get them . . .
I don't know where they are,
but they're here already. *She's* locked them up somewhere.
She won't let us play. She calls it . . .

Ann Laiking about?
T'Devil finds mischief for idle hands to do.
Did your Uncle gie ye owt? Turn them pockets out.
What's pig bank for?
(*Coins put into pig bank*)
Get into your weekday clothes now, both on you.
There's nowt medicine like work.
Which minds me: treacle an' brimstone for both on ye.

Narrator Down our throats went the yellowy-black molasses.

Ann That'll keep your blood clean.

Narrator Ann gave me a long look over the top of her glasses . . .

Ann Tha's fond, lad – but tha's learning.
Weshing up, fetching and carrying,
taking swill to t'pigsty, churning . . .

Narrator I used the only means I knew to vex her
without immediate punishment. I parried
her glance with blankness, which often stirred her
to rap my head, with what she called thimble-pie.
Now she thinned her lips uncertain I'd heard her.

Ann (*Louder than usual*)
Gie Joe a hand in t' stable afore leet's gone.
You're starting schoo-il again, come Monday, think on.
Neville: bedtime, sharp.

Neville (*He's the favoured one*) Yes, Mrs Robinson.
(*The peacock screams*)

Narrator In the late April dusk the small back bedroom
held, like a cup, the lees of the sun's last wine.
The rafters wouldn't have given a tall man head-room.
I went to the window. Over the empty stackyard
I saw the Pointers' brilliant diamonds shine.
Floorboards were chill, then warm to the soles of my feet.
I put my nightshirt on.
Ronald Now Neville kneel beside me.
God bless...
Neville Mummy and Daddy...
Ronald And Uncle Harold and Aunt Ciss and dear Auntie Jess...
Neville And God bless Uncle Jim and Auntie Flo
and Prince and Diamond – and of course Laddie
and Emma. Because I do love Emma so,
she's my favourite pig. And Mr and Mrs Robinson and Pharaoh.
Ronald Very well – but I'm not so sure about Pharaoh.
Neville And God bless you and me.
Ronald This is the important part. Say it very, very carefully and
very slowly:
please, *please* God make Father and Mother better soon.
(*Music – Springlike nocturne – 'Irmelin' by Delius*)
Narrator And Morpheus, smiling, took us in his arms –
held in each other's – before the rising moon
could fill all earth's little children of the night
with ecstasies –
(*Churr-churr of nightjar*)
and tremors and alarms –
(*Sharp bark of vixen*)
the hunted with terror –
(*Shriek of rabbit*)
the hunter with cold delight.
(*Screech of barn owl*)
So, April, weeping, stood aside for May
and I trudged, gladly, two miles every day
in weather warm, wet, dry and cool,
up the hill to North Rigton school –
leaving poor Neville to Iron Ann's misrule.
Lads of the village, who were lads with me,
learned reading, 'riting and the rule of three
from Dominie Dobson, who, so legend sings,

had taught their fathers these salt, basic things –
some said, their grandads, men of pith and ire
who touched their caps to him, though not to squire.
New and a stranger, there I was fair game.

Boy 1 You look like a lass in them curls.

Boy 2 What's yer name?

Ronald (*Reluctant to betray deafness; defensive*)
What did you say?

Boy 1 (*Contemptuous of a weakness*) He's deaf.

Ronald I'm not. I'm stone deaf in this ear. In the other
I can just hear voices I'm used to.

All boys What's yer name? What's yer name?

Ronald I'm Ronald Scriven – and you don't need to shout.

Boy 1 Did yer say . . Crippen?

All (*Delighted*) Crippen! He's Doctor Crippen!

Narrator At bay, I turned upon my chief tormentor.

Boy 2 You've got him mad . . . look out . . .

Narrator Sam Longster, one of the big boys, saw fair play.
They formed an eager circle for the fight.

Boys Hit 'im, Tom. Go on. Give 'im a black eye.

Narrator I took some punches, but I jabbed away
with my left, as Wilfred had taught me in South Milford
and waited to use my right.
A scrap or two – and then I found my level.
Accepted then, in a way I used to revel
in our primitive warfare, fought with sword sticks, clods
and fists, in the dry moat
surrounding what had been an earthwork fortress
when Rigton Hill saw the raven banner float
and Hubba yelled and charged for his pagan gods.
Before the sun quite wearied of the sky
I loitered back. And Ann gave me thimble-pie
– rap, rap.

Ann Kept in? Tha can keep thi breath to cool
thi porridge in't' morning . . .

Narrator Supperless, with ringing head
I went to bed.

Neville Ron. I've kept you a piece of rabbit pie.
I've hidden it. Here it is in Laddie's dish.
She doesn't know.

Oh Ron I wish, I wish Ann'd let me go to school with you.
Ronald Me, too. But she'd only give you oven cake
with nasty fat bacon, or a cold rice pudding to take.
Nev, I've made a new friend.
His name's Alan Church. He gets a Saturday penny
every Saturday.
Neville (*Incredulous*) To spend?
Ronald Every week. On aniseed balls, or a Lucky Packet
with a twist of sherbet inside *and* a football card
and a farthing left over for hundreds and thousands, too.
Neville Wish we had Saturday pennies to buy us spice.
Ronald You're not to talk Yorkshire.
Neville Shall, if I want to. So yah!
Mrs Robinson says we both talk la-di-dah.
Ronald Mrs Robinson? You do – and I'll give you a clip.
So shut up. Look what I've saved for you: a strip
of Everlasting Toffee. Here it is:
Neville It's stuck like glue to your hankie.
Ronald (*Defensively*) Yes I know –
but I only sucked it half an hour or so.
I won it off Alan this afternoon, because
I can always beat him easily at taws.
He's not a meanie – he'd have given it me –
but you mustn't take things if you can't go fair shares, see?
Alan told me a secret.
Neville (*Muffled by Everlasting Toffee*) Go on – tell me, Ron.
Ronald He told me Iron Ann had a son called John
who couldn't stand her – so he ran away to sea.
And *I'd* run away to sea, if it weren't for you.
Neville Don't run away and leave me. Don't! I'll come, too.
Ronald You're too little, Nev. It's as much as you can do
to climb up Wearybones. You'd have your bellyful
if you got to Harrogate – let alone to Hull.
Neville I could!
Ronald Why, it's more than fifty miles away.
I know. I asked Mr Dobson the other day.
Neville I could walk fifty miles.
Ronald You couldn't.
Neville I could. I'm good at walking.
Ronald You're not! You're not!

(*Knocking from below*)
Sh . . . sh . . . She's heard us talking.
(*The peacock screams*)

Narrator So the slow wheel of the seasons broadly turned.
May stood aside for June.
(*Cuckoo*)
The cuckoo changed his tune.
(*Repeat changed tone*)
The morning meadows bathed in thicker dew
which the sun drank with hot delight and burned
more hotly, mopped his brow and drank anew
of water-vapour from the purling beck
which rimmed the Rasser until Joe said . . .

Joe By heck
Glass is set fair. We'll dip us sheep in't morn.

Ann Then lads can take 'levenses. I'se weary-worn.

Ronald (*Aggrieved*) Must I stay off school tomorrow?

Ann Tha mun, an' all.

Narrator Pharaoh was sunning himself on the orchard wall,
his train a-droop like the leaves of the apple trees,
as Slow Joe passed, his shadow at his heels,
and we at Laddie's. Never a breath of breeze
stirred the latest glistening strand of the cobweb wheels
new-spun on the hawthorn hedge.

Neville (*Excited*) Tortoiseshell, tortoiseshell!

Ronald It's a Painted Lady.

Joe Save thi legs, lads, for running after t' sheep.
(*Fade up sheep*)
(*Shouting*) Asta gotten sheep dip ready, Edgar?

Edgar (*Shouting back*) Aye.

Joe (*Normal voice*) Sheep's all ower t' Rasser. We'll have us work cut out.
Lads' legs, like dogs' legs, were made to run about,
soa now's your chance to stretch 'em.

Narrator Joe grinned, and shoved his cap back.

Joe Laddie: fetch 'em.
(*The dog barks*)

Narrator The sheep who did not fear the lion sun
panicked at Laddie and began to run.
He barked, ran, crouched,

rose, ran and barked again.
We tried to head off stragglers, but in vain.

Neville (*Panting*) The stupid stupids!

Ronald Leave those three to Joe.

Neville He never runs.

(*Shepherd's whistle*)

Ronald He whistles to Laddie, though.
Look, between them, they're getting the flock together.

(*The not too distant tingle of a sheep bell*)

They're starting to follow Mary, the bell-wether.
You're sweating more than I am. Don't run any more.

Neville Can't.

Ronald Let's lie down.

Narrator So we flung
ourselves on the lap of earth and watched three score
of thick-fleeced Swaledales bob-bob ever more slowly
while I chewed a blade of Timothy, dry as my tongue.
And the smell of grass and air and sweaty fleece
and happiness, was unutterable peace,
and the smell of earth was holy, holy, holy.

Joe Up, lads!

Narrator A line of willow sallies shaded
a wide, deep pool, at each end barricaded
by wire mesh, slung on ashpoles across the beck.

(*Fade up bleating*)

There Joe and Edgar penned the huddled flock.

Joe Yowes first, then t' lambs. Heave t'owd bell-wether in.

(*Huge splash*)

Narrator Waves, as she floundered, made the surface rock
and like grey seaweed her heavy winter fleece
floated in strands as Edgar thrust her under
with a pronged ashpole. As she rolled and wallowed,
the water was yellowed with oily sheepdip grease.
When he had tubbed her, he let her go, to blunder
towards the sloping bank. The others followed
as Edgar swung the pen gate, one by one.

(*Baa's and splashes*)

Ronald Let's climb along the ashpoles and watch.

Neville Splash, Splash!

(*Splashes and baa's*)

Narrator So Edgar tipped them in by the rump, to send
sun-glittering chip showers of spray
all over our lithe brownness.
(*Splash*)
Ronald Hurray!
(*Splash*)
Neville Hurray!
Narrator Shaking their fleeces like lambs led from the slaughter
the Swaledales dazzled the grass, as swans astonish the water.
Joe Art ready for thi elevenses, Edgar?
Edgar (*With relish*) Aye.
(*The sheepfade*)
Narrator Oven cake, dimpled brown, baked overnight,
Butter, which I had churned and Ann had salted,
Cheese from her dairy, melting, creamy-white,
A great stone jar of foamy nettle beer
of Ann's own brewing, cool, clean, greeny clear:
a feast the pagan gods could not have faulted.
Neville Listen.
Ronald What?
Narrator I saw when he pointed but I couldn't hear.
(*Cuckoo*)
Shouted at, June stepped backwards for July
when cuckoos should, but do not always fly.
July, when school broke up
and stolid rapture brimmed my schoolmates' cup.
(*School let loose*)
Downcast, I dawdled downhill to Low Moor
and pushed aside the half-open kitchen door.
A stranger, a lady, sat in Joe's Windsor chair
with Neville, laughing and talking, in her lap.
Ann We've gotten a visitor. Take off thi cap.
Edith (*Mid-forties, gentle voice, not-quite-a-lady*)
So this is Ronald.
Narrator She had a pale, anaemic countenance
and brown, lacklustre hair.
I understood her grey-eyed gentle glance
and, deep within my being, rebelled at once.
Ann What's up wi' thee? Don't stand gawping like a dunce.
What's happened thi manners? This is Mrs Swaine.

Ronald (*Guardedly*) How do you do?
Edith I came on the afternoon train.
I love Low Moor – and so does Mr Swaine.
I've heard so much about you. Now come and talk to me.
Ronald I've got to take out the pig-bucket.
Ann Nay, let it be.
Sit you still, Edith lass. I'll make us tea.
(*A distant night-jar is heard*)
Narrator In bed with Neville in the night-jarred dusk
we lay long wakeful talking to each other.
The open window breathed in honeysuckle and musk.
Neville I like Mrs Swaine. She has a nice smell. Like Mother.
Ronald (*Vehemently*) No she hasn't. She isn't like Mother one bit.
Neville She is, she is!
Narrator My tongue, half hypocrite,
half outraged loyalist, would not admit
what Neville in his innocence had sensed,
a stranger's mother-instinct; so I fenced
my heart against her until she went away.
Edith Goodbye, Neville.
Neville (*Tearfully*) Goodbye.
Edith I'm coming back a week on Saturday.
Goodbye, Ronald dear.
Narrator I wouldn't meet her eye.
(*Fade up an old-fashioned mowing machine*)
When she returned, Joe's second crop of hay
was bowing before the steady, rhythmic chatter
of the mowing machine, which Prince drew, noddingly,
cut after cut, to a criss-cross, cannibal clatter
to lay the swathes in the pattern of a Greek key.
Sunbonneted, she came with Ann, after tea
just as first heavy raindrops began to patter.
Joe Whoa, Prince!
(*Stop mower*)
By gow, we're in for more'ner a splash.
Ann Edith, us'd best shelter under yon ash.
Run, lads.
(*Rumble up thunder*)
Edith (*Nervously*) Hold my hand, Ronald . . . oh, dear, a lightning flash.
(*Thundery rain falls*)

Narrator From her hand, damp and warm,
I felt fear flowing, and the rain hiss.
Ann What's a-gate, Edith?
It's nobbut a summer storm.
Why, lass, you do look white.
Edith I'm frightened of thunder. Silly, but there it is.
Neville I'm not.
Edith Stand closer, dear. Oh! My strawberries.
I brought them for you and Ronald.
Only a little punnet, but see, they're soaked.
Joe Aye; like my hay.
But I reckon t' sky'll soon clear.
Narrator His weather eye was right. The swathes soon smoked
as the indignant sun came hotspur forth
driving the routed nimbus to the North.
When Mrs Swaine left on Monday, wistful, frail,
she hesitated, turned and lifted her veil
– and I didn't avert my face from her down-stooped kiss.
(*Music – 'Sleigh Ride' by Delius*)
July
died with a summer sigh
breaking
not the school term only, but hard-strained hope.
I saw the postman in the village street
sad-faced, with the dreaded orange envelope.
August that year was the end of a long, long trail
North Rigton men had trodden to Passchendaele.
(*Pause*)
A few more days of heat:
Joe A two three days noo, and I'll cut yon wheat,
glass says 'set fair'
(*Knuckle raps on barometer, interrupted by peacock screams*)
Ann Aye, tha can knock.
Pharaoh thinks different –
and t' peacock's a right storm-cock.
Narrator And August ended in lightning, sheet on sheet
with teeming rain to wreck Joe's standing wheat.
Yet, in a fortnight the world was clean and blithe
and Edgar went in with a whetted scythe

to sweep field-corners clean as a new broom
to give headland-room.
Then I was kept from school, to lend a hand
by tying shocks of corn with hairy band.
Field-labour, once done four whelmed years ago
by strong North Rigton men, brown-faced, aglow –
tall lads, since laid, like nodding poppies, low
in the two bloody battles of the Somme:
lads of the village, Harry, Dick and Tom,
Percy, the gay of heart, and handsome Fred,
whose girls were left to sleep uncomforted.
But the wheel of the seasons rolled
indifferently on.
Cornfields were set with tents of gold.
Blackberries bent the brambles double.
The wayzgoose gleaned the spiky stubble.
Arachne wove her autumn net.
Hazel-nutted, brown October
turnabout was mellow and sober.
Prince and Diamond . . .

Joe Gee there, now . . .

Narrator matched nod and stride before the plough.
November days, with shortening stride
over pasture, ploughland, roots,
in the owl-light, walked beside
Joe, early to his fireside.

Ann Joe? Think on tha scrapes thi booits.

Narrator Joe hooked one thumb in his belt-strap:

Joe Ice in November to bear a duck:
nowt much after but mud and muck.
(*The peacock screams*)

Ann Pharaoh's me weather-cock. There'll be no ice i' November.
– and happen none in December.
Hard winter's still to come.
Which minds me – t' wood shed. Think on?

Joe Awreet, awreet –
I'll fettle t' job tha asks mi, lass. Ti-neet.

Narrator When I'd mucked out the mistal that Saturday,
Slow Joe said:

Joe Sitha.

Narrator There it stood, by Pharaoh's shed:
a soap-box, roughly nailed to a four-wheeled chassis.
I stared at it – my eyes sick-glassy.
Ronald (*Desolate*) *My* motor car!
Narrator Slow Joe had battered
the bodywork to bits and shattered
the headlamps, which had glittered and shone.
Bonnet and rat-trap pedals had gone.
Those pedals, which, one Christmas morn
had thrilled my naked feet from toe to heel
when I scrambled into my car and grasped the wheel,
shouted with joy and poop-poop-pooped the horn.
(*Pause*)
I felt, as Ruth felt in the alien corn:
heartsick for home, forlorn.
Joe There, missus told me to make thi a handy cart
for gatherin' sticks fra hedge bottom.
Narrator At bedtime I told my brother:
Ronald We must say
our prayers specially hard.
Please, please, please God
oh, please make Father better very soon.
Neville And Mother.
Narrator The candle blown out, I saw the text on the wall:
'THOU ART MY ROD AND MY STAFF,'
aglimmer by the light of the hunter's moon.
So the night lengthened swiftly through November.
The cart-rut cat-ice strengthened to bear a duck.
Orion commanded the heavens of December:
The stars of the Dragon were like cold sparks struck
from Diamond's shoe.
Night after night, the Great Bear
was on guard in the frosting air.
Herding the Great Bear and the Little Bear,
Arcturus, the Bear-ward, lit his yellow flare.
So Christmas neared – and I was in despair.
Ronald It's the school breaking-up.
How can I possibly go?
What would she give me to take? Oven cake?
Bacon and cold rice pud. That's Ann. By Jove –

she'd give me dog biscuits to roast on the old school stove.
Neville Awful! I know –
pretend you're sick – and play with me in the barn
in our hidey-hole.
Ronald I will. I'll spin 'em a yarn.
Narrator It seemed to me a simply splendid plan –
but on the Friday morning, Iron Ann
looked over her specs as I put on cap and coat:
Ann I'se packed thi a basket for t' treat. It's summat and nowt.
But it mun do. Hod it carefully, think on.
Narrator I felt like a rabbit when it sees a stoat:
escape there was none.
I went up the cart-track with the wretched thing,
knowing Ann watched me. Lumpiness was spread
with a damped teacloth. Mouldy old bacon and bread
and rice pudding with dates, for a change. I couldn't bring
misery to lift up the cloth and look.
Oh, Ann was sickening. Half-way up the hill
I thought of tipping the lot in the hedge, but Bill
with a basket himself, came running up to hook
his arm in mine.
Bill Just wait until you see what mi' mother's baked.
What's Ann Robi'son gied you?
Narrator What could I say but...
Ronald That's telling. Wait and see.
Narrator Ann's basket was bursting with pastries which melted and flaked:
raspberry jam tarts, rock cakes, lemon curds,
a whole spice cake, some Mazawattee tea,
two bottles of her famous hazel pears
and another of cream and a whole jamboree
of boiled ham sandwiches. Dumbstruck for words
I gloated in the amazement of their stares.
How Ann had known about the treat at all
I no more wondered than the flowers of May
ask why they're born. From wall to schoolroom wall
the strung balloons made my gay heart more gay.
(*Fade up Bobby Bingo, school piano, kid's party row for a moment*)
Joe killed the fatted pig not for my sake.
Not for my sake did Ann set to and bake.

Good measure was pressed down until it overran
to please the peacock pride of Iron Ann.
Yet when I thanked her, hanging up my coat,
she said:

Ann In wartime, summat's better than nowt.
And summat's what I s'll etta find thee to do
now tha's off schoo-il.

Narrator And she found it, too.
Mucking out, churning, forking hay,
feeding pigs and gathering sticks
left me but scant time to play
with Neville, until well turned six.
Then, by the fire, cherryheart-bright
where the peat glowed,
Ann listened and sewed
while I read the Bible by oil-lamp light.

Ann I'll open t' Good Book at t' good Lord's will.

Narrator Leviticus . . . Chronicles . . . Jeremiah.
Deuteronomy . . . Isaiah.
Sometimes, by Ann's bibliomancy,
the great book fell
open where something caught my fancy:
Samson, blinded, at the mill.
Ann nodded her old head, Sybil-wise,
as I read on with clear young eyes.
No oracle there, to indicate
that blindness was to be my fate –
glaucoma took nigh thirty years
to spread from my infected ears.

(*Pause. The pages of a big book are stiffly turned*)

Ronald The mother of Sisera sat by the lattice.
She said: Why tarry the wheels of his chariot?
(*Sudden light, excitedly*) I know, Jael!
She put her hand to the nail
and her right hand to the workman's hammer –
oh, golly!

Ann Naught there for me. I'll open t' good book again.

Narrator Words glittering like stars, half fire, half ice
soon quenched in sleep's deep cup.
Then not the cook, but Ann's voice woke me up:

Ann I've called thee once. I shan't call thee twice.
I'se gotten a job for thee.
I'se going to make us Christmas frumenty.
Narrator The morning sky was black as a moorland tarn.
(*Low up cattle*)
Joe You take the lantern, Ron. We're going to t' barn.
Cold, lad? Then do like me and stamp thi feet.
(*Stamp up feet*)
Sitha, I've putten two shovelfuls of wheat
i' yon sack. Take this flail and bray like 'ell.
Keep on braying away noo, hard and oft
until all t' grain is soft –
or missus 'll bray thee.
(*Wheat flailed*)
Narrator The floury dust rose as the flail rose and fell.
I was warm enough. My arms ached like my back
by the time she came to finger-and-thumb the sack.
Ann It'll do – nobbut. Carry t' sack to t' house.
Narrator Ann went to creed the burst, milk-kernelled grain.
Grandfather's hands . . .
(*Fade up slow tick-tock*)
crept like a wainscot mouse.
A Christmas fly crawled on the window-pane.
So long the dragged-out seconds seemed to me
doing her bidding until long after tea
I thought we scrubbed and polished the kitchen twice.
Next morning she told us:
Ann Make t' fire brisk and hot.
Ron – gan and fetch me t' iron cooking-pot.
– I'se cooking frumenty. Neville – fetch t' allspice,
and t' nutmeg jar and t' ginger jar. Look quick.
And if I catch thi gieing owt a lick –
I'll gie thee thimble-pie *and* warm thi lugs.
Narrator The creeded grain, the colour of raw silk
was tipped into the pot with jugs and jugs
of cream-thick milk.
Ann Now t' raisins – t' musctels. Keep stirring, Ron.
Now – where have I putten yon sticks of cinnamon?
Narrator The rich mess all day long made the kitchen steam
with the fragrance of a paradisal dream.

So our small world wagged, like Grandfather, on,
and Christmas morning came.
Neville (*Urgent excitement*) Ron!
Narrator He was groping in the icy dark.
I hastily lit the candle's tranquil flame.
Neville Our stockings are filled.
I've got a picture book –
oh, oh and a teddy-bear!
Narrator Not the candle, but my eyes flickered. There
in the stocking-top was a bulky box I knew
labelled red, white and blue.
Ronald (*Part exultant, part outrage*) My gun-mule team!
Narrator Three mules with a pair of artillery wheels astraddle;
three with a gun-barrel spring-clipped to the saddle;
one with the ammo to each side, held suspended –
and a leg which Neville had broken and Daddy mended.
Neville Will the guns shoot? Ron, let me have a go.
Ronald (*Brusquely*) No.
Ann's played a trick on us. That's your old teddy-bear.
Neville I know. But I love him, I want him.
Narrator He hugged in joy
all that it meant to him, his long-lost toy.
He was so young, I thought, he's forgotten the rest.
Stumbling downstairs, hand in hand with my little brother,
I clasped, not the box of gun mules to my breast,
but father and mother.
Ann Merry Kersmass.
Narrator She put before my loneliness
a bowl of rich thick appetising mess.
Ann Frumenty.
Narrator Heavenly. And all day, to seduce
my thoughts from home was food: Yorkshire pudding, goose,
high tea with spice loaf, supper with mince pies.
My animal body was in paradise.
My body's soul, having prayed at night-time, wept
and damped the pillow, while my brother slept.
The New Year, like her new moon, came in cold.
January was frosty. Far drums rolled
for old Jarl Winter. Their summoning made Pharaoh
restless upon his perch.

(*The peacock screams*)
Slow Joe said:

Joe Snow.
(*Fade up harsh cold wind*)

Narrator The Viking wind struck from the south-east
cunningly, then came, berserker, from the north
wasting the Southlands till neither man nor beast
dare venture forth.
Besieged, Low Moor was a fortress isolated
by snow-work redoubts, which obliterated
all landmarks, save humped hedges and mantled trees.
The pump was a one-armed snowman, grossly obese.
Joe dug out trenches to mistal, stable and sty.
I followed him, shovelling and scraping.

Joe By!
Now we mun harness Prince to t' snowplough and keep
a clearway up to t' fold to feed yon sheep.
Reckon I took 'em off t' Rasser just in time.

Narrator Morning after morning saw no sun climb
over the snowy rim of Wearybones Hill.
So the month scowled towards its end, until
a low thaw started. The sky was like a school slate
with random scribblings on.
Neville, idly kicking the farm gate,
shouted:

Neville Ron, Ron, Ron!

Narrator A man was coming down the cart-track, blundering
from drift to drift. Sometimes he halted, wondering
whether or not to turn back; but he forged ahead
to shouting distance.

Neville Why, it's the postman, Ted.

Ted Is t' missus about?

Ann She is an' all, lad. I'm none deaf, I heard ye shout.
Kettle's on t' hob. Tha'll be glad of a sup o' tea.

Narrator In her apron pocket, after long scrutiny
she thrust the envelope, gossipped and off he went.
That night Jarl Winter put down the brief mutiny
fiercely – and we were pent
once more in our fortress.
The morning after that

as Joe was dipping bread in his bacon fat . . .
(*A very loud and sudden scream from the peacock*)
the scream, like a soul in hellfire's agony
raised the hair at the back of my neck.

Joe Nay, what the heck . . .

Ann What ails thee, Joe?
It's nobbut t' peacock screaming.

Narrator Out I rushed and there
draggle-tailed on the roof-ridge, glittering against the glare
of the hard-crusted snow: –

Ronald Pharaoh. Pharaoh.
(*Scream up peacock, full-throated*)

Narrator Neville came running. Both of us jigged and danced
screaming back at the peacock as we pranced.
(*Mix peacock with boy's shrieks*)
The more he screamed, the more we both went mad
snowballing him until our hands were numb.
(*Boys' yells*)

Ann Hast lost thi senses? He's screaming for t' thaw to come.
Indoors.

Narrator We *had* lost our senses. We went berserk
and snowballed Ann. She shut the door with a jerk.
(*Door slams*)
Neville and I ran through the farmyard, fighting
a battle in the snow.
(*Scream up peacock again*)
We snowballed Emma. We hammered on doors, exciting
cows, Diamond, Prince – and all the time Pharaoh
screamed from his roof-top.
We tumbled and fought in the hay.
(*Pause*)
At last, exhausted, long after midday
we faced, exultant, the wrath of Iron Ann.
Her mouth was rat-trap, but –

Ann Thi dinner's theer, in t' pan

Narrator – was all she had to say.
Made more foolhardy, I did my worst to provoke
her thimble lightning-stroke
as though inspired by the devil.
I was set back on my heels when she turned on Neville:

Ann I'll box thi ears for thee.
(*Wails from Neville*)
Now: straight ter bed.

Narrator Satan departed from me as suddenly
as Pharaoh's scream had let him into my head.
When Slow Joe lumbered in and had his tea
I did the washing-up.

Ann (*Fairly mildly*) Aye, tha's framed – nobbut. Now sit thi down on t' settle
I'll get mi darning.

Narrator Elbows on table, I read
in silence. Ann, by lamp-light, darned a sock.
So still was the kitchen, I even heard the clock,
old Grandfather:

Clock (*Human voice*) Tick... tock. Tick... tock. Tick... tock.

Narrator There was no rap on the table, no warning cough
but my gaze was drawn towards her face, as though
my name had been sharply named.
She was looking at me over the top of her glasses, steel-framed,
glinting in lamplight. A letter lay on her lap.
Her forehead was wrinkled like the lines of a relief map.

Clock Tick... tock. Tick... tock.

Narrator How draggingly Time sometimes seems to stammer...

Clock (*Dragging it out*) Tick... tock.

Narrator Ann put forth her hand to the nail
and her right hand to the workman's hammer:

Ann I reckon tha'd best know.
Thi mother died last September. They buried thi father
six days ago.
(*Pause*)

Narrator The nail, so unintentionally driven
went through the temples of my childish soul.
I, the I-that-was-I, who had been born
all early in the April and been given
a name, and learned to know it: Ronald Scriven
– the I to whom my father's nod
or loving shake of the head had meant the whole
of what a child can comprehend of God,
and his own relationship to God, was torn
out of my mind. My identity was riven.

What was left of that 'I' felt only passionate
grief for my father and consummate hate
of the God I had trusted. The nail had pierced a hole
in the shield of the sky, which hides from mortal sight
the intolerable light
of the infinite, incomprehensible love of God.
(*Pause*)
Part narrative, part eclogue
and part bucolic, there is an epilogue,
a closing word,
to my story. In my earliest twenties, I heard
by chance, that ill-fortune had come to Iron Ann.
Slow Joe had died. Their son in Canada, John,
had sent her passage money. She had gone
to stay there, penniless . . . In six months she returned,
refusing all save her passage – not to Low Moor
but a two-roomed cottage in Rigton. If she was poor
she scorned to admit it – and illness she scorned, until
they took her to Otley Hospital.
Against my will
I went to see her on a summer day.
The ward was more sad, more grey
for the outside sunlight and smelt of antiseptic
and airlessness and old people, epileptic,
cardiac– life's rage and bones, bedridden.
I went where I was bidden.
There she lay.
Her hair, once screwed so tight
in a bun at the back of her head, was still pure white
but straggled over her shoulders, with a strand
across her specs. With a knotted, bony hand
she pushed the wisp away
and looked at me.
Her eyes were the sort of blue you sometimes see
on an end-of-autumn day.
They knew me instantly, and, as they knew,
the light within them was like the peacock-blue
of Pharaoh's breast.
How could I, how could I, I protest
have known she was dying? She looked so alive

it never entered my head.
Ann (*Old inflexible self, hardly a quaver*)
So tha's come ti see me?
Narrator Ann said.
I stood there, for a moment, without replying.
Ann Asta forgotten how ter bray a frumenty sack?
Narrator I looked, and knew I loved her, and paid her back
in her own iron coin:
Ronald Nay, what's a-gate wi' thee? Tha's non goin' ter dee, lass.
Narrator She cackled with glee, on so prolonged a note,
she all-but brought the death-rattle to her throat.

Dandelion and Parsnip: Vintage 1920

Dandelion and Parsnip: Vintage 1920 was first broadcast on BBC Radio 4 on 2 August 1971 with the following cast:

NARRATOR	*Stephen Murray*
GRANDMOTHER	*Kathleen Helme*
GRANDFATHER	*David March*
JAMES SCRIVEN	*Edward Kelsey*
JESS	*Denise Bryer*
RONALD SCRIVEN	*Judy Bennett*
NEVILLE SCRIVEN	*Jo Manning Wilson*
FRED	*Jean England*
G.B. NEWPORT, M.A.	*Edward Kelsey*
GREAT-AUNT JIN	*Margot Boyd*
GREAT-AUNT SUFF	*Betty Baskcomb*
MR ROBB	*John Rye*
HUGH MILES	*Brian Hewlett*
UNCLE HAROLD	*Nigel Lambert*

Produced by Charles Lefeaux

(*Fade up air: 'My grandfather's clock'*)

Narrator My grandmother's clock was as short as herself
and its voice matched her resonant voice:
(*Single chime of grandmother clock*)

Grandmother As bright was its face
as my best kitchen Delft
and the satiny sheen of its fine walnut case
long, long made my heartstrings rejoice.

Narrator A good Victorian, she had obeyed
her husband's wishes...

Grandfather (*Resigned exasperation*) When it suited her.

Narrator ... in a house where silver gleamed when linen was laid....

Grandmother (*Quiet satisfaction*) And draughts, in the crimson drapes, made
never a stir.

Narrator In that house which to me as a child had seemed so vast,
so full of filtered sunshine, of gaslit glooms,
life moved with a serene, unhurrying glow.

Grandfather No clock, in all my house's many rooms
was ever five seconds fast
– five seconds slow...

Grandmother He liked to believe that.

Narrator I've heard my grandmother say,
who argued with nobody.

Grandfather (*Aggressively*) Certainly not with me.
(*A little puzzled*) I was not as strict as I should have been, maybe.
Somehow, she seemed to go her own sweet way –
though none of our children ever heard her scold.

Narrator In the loomgate of the years, man's memory
is patterned by strands of things he has been told,
criss-crossed by shuttles of family history.
My grandfather, Charles, died in nineteen hundred and nine
when I was two years old.
Over an empire wider than Rome's domain
the Imperial Sun had still some months to shine
on Edward the Seventh's garden-party reign.
(*Pause*)
Decorum drew the blinds in Francis Street.
Slowly, the hooves of the black-plumed horses beat

F

Charles Scriven's last retreat.
(*Funeral horses pass*)
At a decent interval after the will was read,
his eldest son, my Uncle James, surveyed
his father's house, which was now his house and said:

James Well, Mother, no new arrangements need be made.
It won't make any difference when Flo and I
get married in, say, July.
Young Norman's still at college. Ciss and Jess
can run the house while you supervise, more or less
until Flo takes over, after our honeymoon.
Of course, you'll have your own quarters.

Grandmother What, with two unmarried daughters
not to mention a daughter-in-law? No thank you, James.
I'd like a little house of my own. And soon.

James Leave Francis Street? Both Flo and I want you to stay.

Grandmother I've made up my mind. I'll be perfectly content
for Jess to come with me in a *very* small house of my own.

Narrator I hear my uncle's exasperated groan . . .

James (*Exasperated groan*) It's what I've often heard poor Father say:

Grandfather (*Echo from the past*) Don't argue James. She'll go her own sweet way.

Narrator Her own sweet way, my grandmother upped and went –
to a little red box of bricks James bought for her.

James Number Six, Baldovan Terrace, Harehills.
(*Heavy jocularity*) You've got a kettle to tick and a cat to purr.
No rent to pay – and Jess will watch the bills.

Grandmother And I'll watch Jess.

James (*Uneasy at suspected sarcasm*) Eh?

Jess (*Nineteen. Very capable. Eager and loving*)
Oh, mother dear, we'll all look after you.

James Is there nothing at all you want from Francis Street?

Grandmother (*Chuckles*) If you both insist – I'd like my old broad crock.
Too big – but it keeps new-baked bread moist and sweet –
especially when the flour's been stone-ground.
(*Slight pause*) Oh – and perhaps young Jess will miss the sound
of my old grandmother clock.
(*Fade up ticking grandmother clock*)

Narrator By 1920 my grandmother, in the prime
of her old age and the ease of her widowhood,

stood a little sauce from Jess, but none from Time.
I think she sensed it as a rhythm in her blood,
like weeks, months, seasons – and the longer stride
which yet she scarcely noticed, of the years.
She never argued with them; nor did they
argue with her. She went her own sweet way,
having long since done with tears.
If she wept, she wept in her old heart, grieving for
her second son, my father, when he died
in the last year of the '14 – '18 war,
six short months after my mother's early death:
a double blow, which crushed my childish faith
in a God to whom I'd nightly said my prayers
and in whose love I trusted, as in theirs.
Neville, my brother, four years younger than I,
was spared the full weight of the blow, protected by
his shorter memory, from the most piercing harm.
(*The peacock screams*)
What was that sound? I hear it still, in dreaming.
Ann Nay, nobbut peacock screaming.
Narrator The voice of Iron Ann, of Low Moor Farm,
into whose care,
believing that, in war-time, country fare
would build our bodies up, and fresh air brace us,
my Uncle James had been well pleased to place us.
Ann, to whom, in the snowbound farmhouse, I'd read
the story of Jael before I went to bed,
(*The peacock screams*)
the day I was startled by the peacock's clamour:
Ann put forth her hand to the nail
and her right hand to the workman's hammer.
How could I know she'd pondered what to say,
hour after hour in her groping mind,
then blurted by lamplight, meaning to be kind...
Ann Tha'd best know. They buried thi' father yesterday.
(*Distant brief artillery barrage*)
Narrator That summer of the bloodiest war's climax,
the storm of steel, the big putsch, the gas attacks,
passed, for me, like a chiaroscuro dream
rent by Pharaoh, the peacock's recurrent scream,

yet flower-shot with beauty, with the gleam
of the spread peacock-fan.
In solitude I wandered Wearybones Hill
seeking enchanter's nightshade, watching the play
of cloud-shadows under a sun like a burning glass.
I saw the grass-snake's movements make the grass
ripple against the wind, as the kestrel saw, the wrong way.
I knew no more what was happening to me than
I knew the voice within me which said:

Voice Be still.

Narrator You knew, before I was born; you knew, Housman.

Housman The earth, because my heart was sore,
Sorrowed for the son she bore;
And standing hills, long to remain,
Shared their short-lived comrade's pain.

Narrator But summer passed, as summers pass
whichever way wind blows the grass
and at its end our guardian
James, rescued us from Iron Ann:

James You're going to live with your grandmother.

Narrator Into that placid backwater, my brother
and I went plunging, like pike in a still millpool.

Jess Hello, dears.
(*Two auntly kisses*)

Ronald (*Very loudly: he's rather deaf*)
Look, Neville. Iced walnut cake for tea.

Neville (*Much more quietly, but excited*) Fruit salad.

Jess Don't shout, Ronald dear – it upsets Mother.
(*Gently*) We know you're deaf, but she's not.

Grandmother All boys are noisy – they won't upset me a jot.
Come and give me a kiss.

Ronald (*Ultra-quiet, by no means subdued*) Yes. Grandma.
(*Kiss*)
How are you? I thought we were going to stay
at Milford, with Uncle Harold and Auntie Ciss.

Jess (*Sparkling a little; she and her mother have had a tiff over it*)
Yes – and so you would, if I'd had my way.
We're moving house. Day after tomorrow.

Ronald (*Great enthusiasm, shouting again*) I say.

Neville Where are you moving, Grandma?

Ronald Are we going to live at Scarbro'? Like Great-Uncle John?

Neville Oh, oh, I'd love to live by the sea for ever and ever.
Wouldn't you, Ron?

Jess Well, you're not going to. Your grandmother's beating a very short retreat.
(*Dryly*) We're only moving to Number Three, Ellers Road.

Ronald (*Even he is startled*) Well, I'll be blowed!

Narrator Ellers Road and Baldovan Terrace shared the same cobbled back street.
Number Three was exactly opposite Number Six.
Each row of houses was built of identical bricks.
Each house of each row had been built to the same Victorian plan
by the same builder, with solid, Victorian pride.
There wasn't a pin to choose between them all
from chimney pot to cellar, attic to hall,
they were painted the same dull shade of old-mustard-brown,
Except for the people inside.

Ronald *Why*, Grandma?

Narrator My Uncle James came galumphing down
that afternoon. With a massive, buffalo frown
he asked the same question.

Jess It's no use asking her, Jim.

Narrator But he did, with emphasis, twice.

Grandmother I've made up my mind.

Narrator My grandmother smiled at him.
He tugged at his collar. His temper was peppery-hot.
The only answer the pair of them ever got was:

Grandmother Because of the draughts and the mice.

James Draughts? I've been round every door, every window-frame:
There isn't a draught to flicker a candle flame.

Jess Mice?
(*Indignantly*) There's never a mouse in the house.

Grandmother (*Darkly*) Mice always come from next door – and they never go back.

Narrator My uncle gave his knee an impatient smack,
lost on his mother, who sailed gaily on:

Grandmother I've ordered two new carpets – from the Grand Pygmalion.
A nice blue Wilton, for the parlour. That old and shabby one
was faded by the sun.
A plain Axminster, for my bedroom. Sage.

James (*Incensed*) What? You'll not get the value out of them, Mother,
Not at your age.
Jess (*Shocked*) James!
Grandmother (*Not in the least shocked*)
They've already been delivered. I'll send you the bills.
James Mother: you'll be the laughing-stock of all Harehills.
Grandmother Turnbull's removing me. A very nice man.
Most reasonable. They won't of course, need a van.
He says his men can carry my bits of sticks
directly across the road from Number Six.
So, James, I'll pay him out of my current account.
James (*Conceding defeat*) Send me the bills. I'll settle the whole amount.
Don't think for a moment, Mother, that I approve.
I'll take these boys with me to Francis Street
for the rest of the holidays, while you remove.
Narrator We groaned internally.
Grandmother You'll do no such thing.
I know you mean well – but as for the trouble – why
I'll have my heart's desire.
Narrator The day of her heart's desire dawned.
Neville and I, in the attic, yawned –
then tumbled out of bed, as though
Christmas morning had come, with snow.
We rushed to the window, with one glad cry:
Neville Mackerel sky! Mackerel sky!
Ronald (*Shouting with enthusiasm*) Not long wet, not long dry!
Jess (*Downstairs calling up, sarcastically*)
Is the house on fire? Hi!
Stay in bed till I call you.
Both (*Groaning*) Oh!
Narrator Long minutes limped by, lead-foot slow.
Neville She's forgotten us.
Narrator Aghast,
we stayed, whilst endless time flowed past.
(*Furniture is dragged about in other rooms*)
Neville Bumps, Ron!
Ronald Bashes. Crashes. Blow –
get your clothes on. Let's not wash.
She'll never notice.
Come on: downstairs.

Neville We'd better comb our hair –
(*Door open*)
oh, gosh.

Ronald Mattresses. Pillows. Chamber-pots, chairs.

Neville Books. That broken birdcage. Pictures.
Frying-pans and sheepskin mats.
And dozens of bonnets, hundreds of hats!

Narrator Little we heeded Jess's strictures:

Jess Here. Keep out of the way, you two.

Remover 1 Steady, Bert. From me to you.

Remover 2 Mind them steps. From you to me.

Remover 1 Heave.
(*Sharp wooden crack*)
It's only the leg of that settee.

Narrator Mad as March hares, we hopped and skipped about
in and out of the moving, green baize daisy chain.
In half an hour...
(*Heavy rain*)

Jess It would!

Narrator ... down came the rain.

Grandmother (*Calling across from new house*)
Jess – the men have left my piano out in the street –
oh, my new carpets. Ask them to wipe their feet.

Remover 1 (*Shouting from the street in kind, common-sense British Working Kid tone*) Lady, we always moves them door-mats last
– especially in weather like this.

Jess (*Calling back*)
Surely the men put dust-covers over them, Mother?

Remover 2 (*Similar kind type, beside Jess, exasperated by the folly of women*) In course we did. But then the old lady, Miss, wanted to
look at 'em, first in one room, then t'other
and what with them kids and one thing and another...

Jess (*Moaning*) You forgot to put the dust sheets back again.
(*Turning her anger on to boys*) You two...

Grandmother (*Coming to Jess vexed with herself*)
It's my fault, not theirs. They were only showing willing.
You've got my purse, haven't you? Give them each a shilling.

Both (*This is real money*) Oh, thank you, Grandma!

Ronald Grandma: may we go to The Parade?

Grandmother You may.

Jess You bet you may.
Now ... where did I put those sandwiches I made?
(*Fade up 1918 traffic*)

Narrator On The Parade, the shop of shops
was Harold Wimpenny's. Behind
its flyblown window, to spellbind
the souls of boys, we'd always find
a rich confusion of delights.

Ronald Water pistols. Paper kites

Neville Ouija Boards. Ping-pong balls. Peg tops.

Ronald Bull's eyes. Everlasting toffee strips.

Neville Wine gums. Victory V's. Lollipops.

Ronald Pea-shooters – and monkey nuts.

Narrator Wimpenny knew those went together.

Neville Chips and The Rainbow. Bags I Chips.

Narrator Warmly we debated whether
to go for Chips, or Comic Cuts?
Weary Will and Tired Tim –
or the bad lads of Casey's Court.

Neville (*Insisting*) Chips.

Ronald Sexton Blake.

Neville I don't like him. Chips is funny.

Narrator A mort of thought when spending money.
He gave a boy-of-action's grin,
pushed his cap back and dashed in.
In Neville's pockets, money burned.
He rushed back, whistling.

Neville Ron – look what I've got – a seebackroscope,
(*Suddenly wildly exited*) I can see backwards all the way up The Parade.
People – and trams – and shops – Wormald's, Gosney's, Scarr's –
butcher's vans, baker's vans, bikes – and three motor cars.

Ronald (*Crisply*) Gimme.

Neville Shan't. I bought it. It's mine. It cost me a tanner.

Narrator I tried to grab his ear, but off he made.
I had the speed, he, the Artful Dodger manner.
He sidestepped old ladies –

Old lady (*Shriek of reproach and alarm*)

Narrator Skipped around boxes and crates.

(Clatter of overturned boxes)
He nipped round corners as though on roller-skates.
Looking ahead – and through the seebackroscope –
he went like a bird in a panic –
he cannoned into a postman, ricocheted – missed a mechanic.
Girls shrieked, dogs barked, I, hollering and whooping after
spurred by anger and pulled on the curb of my laughter,
and saw that he hadn't a hope.
I was almost on him, intent on thumping his head,
when a bigger boy grabbed me:

Fred *(Not hostile)* So it's you ,yer young bugger.

Ronald *(Joy)* Fred! Our paper-boy. From Harehills Avenue.

Fred *(15 to Ronald's 13: very hard-bitten. Dreadfully up against it)* Ay. Gie us five Woodbines.

Ronald *(Embarrassed by shameful admission)* I don't smoke.

Fred One'll do.
Or a tab end.

Narrator I looked away. Fred, who had been my friend,
was grimy, ragged, in clothes that were all the wrong size
and too tight at the bony wrist.
He looked frail as a ghost
and – this shocked me most –
with neither boots nor shoes on his scrawny feet.
How could I guess that the hunger in his eyes
was past hunger for food; it was hunger for nicotine.
I was ashamed of being ashamed to meet.
Fred wasn't ashamed. He gave a shrug – and a twist of his wry mouth.

Fred *(Quite blithe: he's seen changes)* Aye. Yer used to live in the Avenue
with yer father and mother. Ow are they doing?

Ronald *(Suddenly dead-pan voiced and harder than Fred)*
They're dead.

Fred Aye? *(Disaster in his world is taken for granted)*
Yer'll be living with yer grandma, I reckon.
The one that got pissed
and bought half t'oranges in Leeds City Market.
She used ter sing: Ta-ra-ra-BOOM-de-ay.

Ronald *(More at ease)* With my other grandmother – she's not a bit like the one you knew.

Fred D'yer pinch much from her?

Ronald (*As shocked as by his first reaction*) Of course not.
Fred Nark it.
Ronald (*Defence of his own, as well as of his integrity*)
Grandma Scriven is very generous.
Neville (*He's been hovering*)
You bet. She gave us a bob each only this morning.
Look. I bought this seebackroscope with half of mine.
Narrator Fred looked at him with a glance of incredulous scorning.
Fred Yer paid good brass fer that?
Neville It was jolly good value, Fred.
With a seebackroscope you can see everything behind you.
Fred Yer bloody cawf-head. Yer've nobbut ter turn yer 'ead.
Narrator No words could express the contempt with which he spat.
Neville (*Hurt*) You don't understand.
Fred Use yer loaf.
Mi feyther always tell't me:
Father Folk as lives on one side o' Leeds Bridge
dizzn't know how folk on t'other side on it live.
Fred S' a fact. Yer know no more than a bloody midge.
See this clobber I'm wearing?
I got a right good suit yesterday. From t' nuns.
Ronald Then why aren't you . . . ?
Fred Cos I flogged it.
If I don't take owt I can get to my uncle's,
mi feyther wouldn't half belt me.
Ronald He must be a wicked uncle.
Fred (*Crowing with contemptuous laughter*)
He keeps a pawn-shop – aye, and t' pawn-shop keeps him.
Narrator The penny dropped.
My blood
thickened suddenly,
was quickened
by the feeling, straight from God, of brotherhood.
Yet I hesitated, having too thin a skin.
Neville plunged in:
Neville Take these.
Four farthings . . . a penny . . . two ha'pns and a threpp'ny bit.
Ronald (*With a rush*) And this bob
– I'm afraid we've eaten our sandwiches,
but here's an apple –

(*Apologetically*) I've only taken a bite out of it.

Fred (*Collectively, in every sense, no emphasis*) Ta.

Narrator Fred
thumped his chest, with the fingers of one bony hand outspread –
I can see them now – to check a cough,
grinned, and was off.

Ronald (*Put out, baffled as he sees it by having his good intentions flung back in his face*)
Fred. Fred, come back...
We're friends, Fred, aren't we?

Fred (*Calling down the wind, floatingly, jeeringly*) Yah!
(*Pause*)

Narrator Dusk came to the city. A strange, chill, magic, shy light
in which vague blue, deepening violet colours swirled.
A mysterious, troubling, early April twilight.
Homewards we went, brushed by its spell, and found
the household gods of our small, immediate world
ill at their ease and turned the wrong way round.

Grandmother My pictures. My carpets...

Narrator Jess watched her wandering.

Jess (*Reassuringly*) The parlour faces the sun.

Grandmother There'll be too much glare.
How can I lay my hands on a single thing
when my kitchen cupboards are *there* instead of *there*?

Narrator We went to bed.

Neville (*Giggling*) The attic's the wrong way round.

Narrator He slept as soon as the pillow touched his head.
But the stars troubled me and I could not sleep.

Ronald (*To himself*) Fred.

Narrator He had come, like a ghost, from holy ground
my thoughts refused to tread.
Wretched, confused, I stared into the deep,
the lonely, the unutterably profound
chasms of space.
Only at this remoter, later date
do I attempt, now, to translate
ideas, gropings inchoate,
remembered feelings, into words.
Then the mystery of night
was washed away by morning light

to the Te Deum of the birds.
(*Birds sing and sparrows cheep*)
Beside me, Neville sucked a forbidden thumb.
Ronald Are you awake?
Neville M'mmm.
Narrator The sparrows' cheep ... cheep ... cheep
drifted us back upon the tide of sleep
as the sun began to climb.
At the other end of the swing of the pendulum
we were, like our grandmother, on easy terms with time.
Grandmother Clock (*Human voice – slowly*)
Tick ... tock ... tick ... tock.
Narrator Then, with a doom-stroke shock:
(*Clock chimes the half-hour*)
Ronald I say. The end of the holidays has come.
Narrator Oh Toffee Town, carpet town,
Hilly, chilly Halifax,
which blackens, from tall chimney stacks
nine more than Rome's seven hills.
Town of machine tools, factories, mills,
of carpet works and gibbet axe.
The Middle Ages, lustily,
sang of it this litany:
Chorus From Hull, Hell, and Halifax
Good Lord, deliver us!
Narrator Victorian philanthropy
ground the faces of the poor
(meekly grateful, as a rule)
to crown the crest of Savile Moor
with a noble edifice (thrice
removed from its original:
a palace on the Grand Canal)
the Nonconformist conscience
embodied foursquare: Crossleys School.
The headmaster, a man of parts,
was:
Newport G.B. Newport, Master of Arts.
Narrator A scholar of Caius, an Anglo-Indian,
a grave, plump, still athletic man –
for how could any man of parts forget

he'd once kept amateur wicket
for Somerset?

Newport (*Blandly*) Just so.

Narrator He governed the boys' school and rectitude governed his paths.
His subjects were:

Newport (*A shade pompous*) Scripture. Latin. Chemistry. Maths.

Narrator (*Mock sadness*) Nothing he taught me set my mind aglow.
I stumbled for knowledge as one blindfold through a thicket
knowing not which way to go.
Guv made allowances for my deafness, at least.
He was fond of quoting:

Newport A beast, but a just beast.

Narrator It was said of him:

Sixth-form boy: Guv has three gods, you know –
God, Kipling and cricket.

Narrator I hugged that saying to my breast with joy
in moments of disaster.
A wise man said:

Voice It takes a master ten years to know a boy.
It takes a boy ten minutes to know a master.

Narrator Although, from the first, I was aware of him,
as were all beneath his rule,
it took me two years merely to learn to swim
among the small fry of the lower school.
Two years of a boy's life pass like a boy's dream,
fleeting, fleeting,
gone as soon as he opens his eyes
to the new day, whether of downcast skies
or the dawn-chorus, greeting
the new sun's molten gleam.
From August 1918 to Easter 1920
seemed but a sleep overnight,
from which I started
to hear my brother shouting with delight:

Neville Ron! Ron!

Narrator My heart was singing like a linnet
knowing that from now on,
each hour, each minute
was mine, crammed with God's plenty.

Neville I've got a kinematograph, I've got a kinematograph,

with films of galloping horses n' express trains.
It's got a real lamp n' the chimney smokes –
only Aunt Jess won't let me use it till tonight.
I've got a box of jokes
that make you laugh –
only grandma didn't when she smelled a smell like the drains.
And when the drains really did smell, Aunt Jess blamed me.
Have you got any new cigarette cards?

Ronald Yes. What's for tea?

Neville I've not to tell you.

Narrator His eyes were dancing bright
and teasing titillated appetite.

Ronald (*Raising voice*) Seedy cake? Walnut cake?

Neville No. It's something hot.

Ronald Bet it's salt horse and hard tack,
crawling with maggots.

Neville It isn't then – it's faggots.

Ronald (*Shouting*) With spotted dog for afters.

Jess Now take your bag to the attic and unpack.
And mind the two of you have a thorough wash.

Ronald I can smell a rabbit pie in the oven. Gosh
my mouth is watering already.

Neville Yes. So's mine.
She's making the gravy with grandma's elderberry wine.

Ronald Great-aunt Jemima makes dandelion wine. Wonderful.

Neville You've never . . .

Ronald Yes, I have. Last Christmas night.
She let me taste it when I held her knitting wool.

Jemima There. One spoonful in the bottom of the glass.
More potent than Imperial Tokay.

Neville (*Aside*) What's that?

Ronald (*Aside*) The Chinese name for dandelion wine, you ass.

Jemima If I gave you a whole glassful . . .

Ronald Aunt Jemima said,

Jemima . . . you'd go out like a light.

Narrator (*Chuckling*) I'm perfectly certain that the old girl was right.

Ronald And then, on New Year's day,
Great-aunt Suff let me taste her parsnip wine. Yum, yum.

Suff It's stronger . . .

Ronald she said,

Suff ... than Demarara rum.
If you drank a whole bottle, you'd be drunk till Kingdom Come.

Neville (*Impressed: with conviction*)
We'll be squiffier than newts when we've eaten that rabbit pie.

Narrator His prophecy was fortunately rash.
The holidays passed like a kingfisher-lightning flash
zigzagging over a brook.
On the last day but one, my grandmother took
from a locked kitchen cupboard a great stone bottle
as portly as an abbot.

Grandmother Harry Holgate's stone gingerbeer.

Narrator Fiery-cool, green-foaming, clear
Harry Holgate's gingerbeer
was surely made in heaven, to quench
a merely mortal thirst.
We drank and drank... We made Jess blench.

Jess I know those boys will burst.
They will if you touch 'em with a pin.
Are you sure you've had enough?

Ronald Yes – it's empty.
Please, Grandma, may I go and see Great-aunt Jin – and Great-aunt Suff?

Jess How dutiful of you, Ronald. Are you broke?

Ronald It's surprising how soon a chap runs short of tin.

Grandmother (*Laughing*) It's a shame to call the poor boy's bluff.
Be off with you. Here, give him his tram-fare, Jess.

Narrator Was her smile meant to chide me, or to tease?
To approve, or disapprove? My fingers grope
unsure, for memory's cracked seebackroscope.
The way the sunlight played over her glasses and made
the rims strike goldy glisters
like the glints in her Irish eyes
comes back to me, heliograph-wise,
over the bridge of sighs,
of grief and gladness and tears,
which spans the gulf of the years.
Sophia and Jemima were her sisters,
who covertly pursued
a pious, silk-and-satin, lace-edged feud

of endless tittle-tattle skirmishings.
At weddings, funerals, christenings,
bazaars and puttings-up of banns
they pinked each other's partisans
with delicate, skilful, pointed stings.
How was I to know which way
who thrust, who parried, or cried:

Jin Touché.

Narrator The long path to Jin's garden door
was bordered by dandelions galore.
A walking dumpling, in gold specs
and a gingham apron in blue-and-white checks
answered my ring. My great-aunt Jin.
(*Door opens*)

Jin (*Far from cordial*) Oh! It's you, Ronald. Well – come in.
Wipe your feet and blow your nose.
(*Abruptly*) You've seen your Great-aunt Suff, I suppose?

Ronald (*Voice ringing with truth*) No, Aunt Jemima. I've come to see you.

Jin (*Instant change to sweetness and light*)
How nice of you, Ronald. Come along, dear.
The sun's on the window-seat. Sit down, do.

Ronald (*Eagerly*) Please, may I look at the *Evening Post*?
(*Crackle of newspaper*)
Yorkshire's a hundred and ninety for three.

Jin Are they, now? (*Calling loudly*) Ethel.

Ethel (*Calling back*) Yes, Mama?

Jin Tea.
Salmon salad. Pears. Cream cake. Lashings of toast.
Set about it. Dear Ronald's here.
(*Lower, sharp tone*) Ida, put down that Marie Corelli.
Bring out the last of my crab-apple jelly.

Ida (*Reluctantly*) Yes, Mama.

Narrator That was a tea worth waiting for.

Ronald Bet Holmes makes a thousand runs in May.
The first real season since the war.
Bet they'll be champion county. Hurray!

Jin Yes, dear. Now put that paper away.

Narrator My snake-belt tighter than before,
in half an hour I had to pay
my dues to nature. When I came down

I kissed my aunt and hooked it, gay,
my pocket the richer by half a crown.
A double –
(*Sharp double knock*)
– and open flew Aunt Suff's door.
(*Door opens quickly*)
Great-aunt Suff's hair was grey and bingled.
She was thin as a hawk and in her eyes,
sharper than a hawk's, were mingled
– was it suspicion? Delight? Surprise?

Suff (*Cordiality just short of gush*)
Ronald! How lovely to see you. Come in.
How's your dear grandmother? And *dear* Aunt Jin?
You've been to see her, haven't you?

Ronald Yes. She's very well, thank you.

Narrator She let this fall,
like a hawk which stoops on a mouse
and, disgusted, finds it a shrew.
Her change of manner ill-concealed
she marched me from her chilly hall
to a chillier room at the back of the house.

Suff (*Cold-snap voice*) Sit down. Read David Copperfield.
(*Tone of grudging hospitality*) I'll see what sort of a tea I can make.

Narrator The feast Great-aunt Jin's rival spread
might have made Billy Bunter quake.
Galantined tongue and breadcrumbed ham,
home-made brawn, three kinds of jam,
Sally Lunns, teacake, white bread, brown bread,
cream-filled Queen Mary's chocolate cake.
What filled me with consternation
was Aunt Suff's cough-drop conversation.

Suff Why put those cherries on the edge of the plate?

Narrator she said.

Ronald Because I like them best.

Narrator That sealed my fate.

Suff Eat them at once, or God may strike you dead
before you reach them.

Narrator Three gulped cherries seemed, oddly, to placate
my aunt's mysterious wrath.
She smiled, if frostily, at the juice-stained cloth.

She gave me two half-crowns at the garden gate.

Jess Well, Ronald – any luck with the Jameson raid?

Ronald What do you mean, Aunt Jess?

Jess Never mind. Your grin announces its success.
D'you think you can face the farewell tea we've made?

Ronald (*Enthusiastic*) M'mmm.

Jess What, didn't they throw in tea with their largesse?
How on earth do boys keep their bodies attached to their souls?

Neville I'm going to school with you next term, Uncle James says
Won't it be ripping to be together *always*?

Ronald (*Perfunctory*) Topping. Grandma, I've got a new friend, Hugh Moles.
Hugh's in the fifth. He's brainy. He's ever so thin.
He can run like a hare. Hugh always wins the mile.
He can run for hours on end and never tire.
Robb – he's our English master – says Hugh has style
and was made of whipcord and piano wire.

Neville Ron, Ron, Aunt Jess is taking us to the flicks.
Ruth Roland – spiffing – and the Keystone Cops.

Ronald (*Much more interest*) What's the big picture?

Neville Cowboys and Indians. Tom Mix
and his pony, Tony.
Ron, next Saturday, it's Rin-Tin-Tin
at the Harehills Cinema.

Jess (*Tolerant sarcasm*) Where plutocrats like Neville can always get in
for – what is it, Neville?

Neville (*Seriously*) Two jam jars – or a rabbit skin.

Narrator Ruth Roland lashed to the rails, while an express train
attacked by Red Indians in the pouring rain
confused the camera of my sleeping brain
that night, to make the pulse of the nightmare leap.
Then I plunged – with but that intervening sleep –
from the cool, backwater world of woman's rule
into the rapids of the middle school.
I knew I must fight my way upstream, among
the chubby, grubby teeming finny race,
the roach, the barbel bullies, the weak and the strong,
the placid perch, the lively-darting dace,
the jostling, shoulder-to-shoulder mostly tame fish.
And here and there the colourful, fighting game fish

The rainbow trout amidst the duller shoals.
Masters of their ruthless art, water bailiffs from the banks,
netted us, sorted us apart and plopped us into classroom tanks.
(*The school hand-bell rings*)

Master 1 Maths.
(*Bell*)

Master 2 Latin.
(*Bell*)

Master 3 Geography.
(*Bell*)

Master 4 Chemistry.

Narrator Stinks.
Once Coleridge, when in Cologne, counted:

Coleridge (*Fierce disgust*) Two and seventy stenches.

Narrator I was no longer an indeterminate blob
in the spawning shallows of the lower school.
I was a personality, an entity.
My deafness gave me an undesired identity –
and a wide reputation as a fool.
I never heard more than a word or two in class.
Yet all the masters who taught me knew their job.
Though I stayed on this side of the bridge, with Euclid's ass,
Guv – that just beast – never treated me as a mule.

Newport (*Old-fashioned, academic, authoritative, slightly pompous*)
You're going to get matric in two or three years.
I'll give you special attention.

Narrator All my fears
quivered – and almost literally, my ears.

Newport Maths...

Narrator I equated maths with misery.

Newport ...and another weak point of yours: chemistry.

Narrator My nerves were galvanised. My spirits sank.
Stinks. How they stank.
(*Grudging admiration*) And he kept his word, the nabob.
I hobbled: I was always out of step.
One afternoon the English master, Robb, said:

Robb Scriven. Come and see me after prep,
in the Masters' Common Room.

Narrator I tapped on the door, a hollow sound of doom.

Robb (*Manchester Grammar School; very pleasant voice:*

coughs at appropriate intervals)
(*Beyond door*) Come in. Ah, Scriven. Take a pew –
that leather one, as Mr Hanson isn't about.
Just thought I'd have a bit of a chat with you –
get a few things sorted out.

Ronald (*Nervy*) Y-yes, sir.

Robb This essay of yours on the coal measures . . .

Ronald (*Jumping in to ward off anticipated criticism*)
Please sir, the statistics . . .

Robb You dug out of the Enc. Brit. in the library, no doubt.
A line of comment – then, from something you've read –
do I smell the pages of Guerber's Ancient World? –
you up and dive straight into the Book of the Dead,
apostrophise Thoth, the god with the bird's head –
imagine, like the old Egyptian mystics
(*Pages of book turned*)
– here we are –
'how richly the blue smoke of incense curled
to please the gods, from the temples of the Nile.'
All very heady stuff, but on the whole,
though I see how you got there, a shade remote from coal.

Ronald (*Extremely dashed*) I'm sorry, sir.

Robb (*Energetically*) Sorry? There's the stuff of poetry in it.
A hundred such essays are duller than unwashed coal.
Yours reads as though it might burst into flames any minute.
Mind you, the most splendid words need the most control.
Read your dictionary as though it were Holy Writ.
Beauty is truth, truth, beauty, Keats said. To the right eyes
there are both, my boy, in the slag heaps spewed from a pit.
Use your eyes to see, as well as to read, if you're wise.

Ronald Yes, sir. Please sir, what ought I to read –
apart from the dictionary, I mean?

Narrator I see his face. See each sweat-bead
on his yellowy skin, where the line of his hair
framed his wide forehead. See the lean
hollow cheeks, the generous span
of his mouth, all quirks, a Shakespearean clown's.
His eyes smiled, even when twitching frowns
betrayed the pain he had to bear.
Robb was sick, a courageous man,

once far from physically frail.
Hugh Moles told me Robb had been
shell-shocked and gassed at Passchendaele.

Robb (*Slight cough here*) Read? Everything with life and breath.
Penny dreadfuls – the Tale of Troy –
shilling shockers, like Macbeth –
Bevis: the story of a boy.
Hitch your waggon to any star
which draws you, whether by land or sea.
(*Strong sucking noise*) My pipe's out. Scriven – be a good chap –
push over that tobacco jar.

Narrator I sprang from Hanson's leather chair:

Ronald There's something on top of it.

Narrator Robb sprang his trap:

Robb Now who on earth can have put that there?
H'm. Palgrave's Golden Treasury.
Read poetry? This is a capital thing.
You may borrow it. On second thoughts, no:
lent books are never homers – so:

Narrator He scribbled the fly-leaf...
(*Scrawl of pen*)

Robb Off you go.

Narrator Poetry is for kindred souls.
I showed the inscription only to Moles.

Hugh (*Reading. He's 16 to Ronald's 13*)
'Drink deep, or taste not the Pierian spring'.

Narrator Unawares, on many an arduous hike
with Hugh to Norwood Edge, or Studley Pike,
I drank from rivulets of that spring, in ghylls
cleft among roots of burnt heather high in the hills
where it was sweet to rest
and talk the jumbled-rainbow talk of youth
which does not guess that the crock of gold, in truth,
brims out of the flowering gorse
as the linnet sings –
runs over where a beck hare-leaps its watercourse
from side to side down never-wet, never-dry rocks.

Hugh Look, Ron – yellow hill-fox.

Ronald Where? Now I see him.

Hugh He's stalking.

Narrator Hugh yelled, with zest:
(*War-whoop*)
Hugh There. That's sent him streaking for the dry wall.
Hope he thinks the hounds are on his track.
(*A faint alarm call of grouse*)
Listen! Can you hear the red grouse call?
Grouse (*In distance*) Go back. Go back.
Narrator Hugh started up. His gaze
was always on the hills, on the next crest.
He talked, as he walked, fast.
I toiled after him.
Ah, those were glorious days,
when the sun shimmered through the faint blue heat-haze
and the sky was vast and the future still more vast
– to me, vaguely, rosily dim
– to Hugh, clear as the sky over Ararat
when Noah let down the gangway from the ark.
He knew exactly how he would make his mark
and with what ease.
Hugh I'll take a scholarship, see if I don't, to Caius –
I'll take an honours degree and after that
get a post in the Chinese Secretariat
in Kuala Lumpur.
And you know what that means.
Narrator Did Hugh's eyes, ranging the future, see
beyond the Chinese Secretariat and the swarm
of peoples and creeds and colours and the long years
of learning their ways and languages – suddenly
the bursting of the yellow storm
out of Japan? The blood, toil, sweat and tears
which whelmed whole nations in the war-typhoon?
Did he see himself organising, in Rangoon,
a convoy of five trucks of refugees
to take to the jungle, with the Japanese
all round him and the length of Burma ahead?
He reached Assam with one truckload, most of them dead or
dying.
I've seen a photograph of him: death's own head,
so tight was his skin, what you could see of it, under the spread
of the beard matted to his eyeball sockets.

Did he foresee *that* as he talked to me, hands in pockets?
His mother sent me that photo, with the news that he lived.
He was awarded some civilian gong.
I thought, as I read her letter, of the long
whipcord and piano-wire, frail-seeming
figure of the Hugh who was my friend.
A lap between the field and Hugh at the start
of the school mile – a lap between Hugh and the field
at the mile's end.

Hugh Yes, get a post in the Chinese Secretariat in Kuala Lumpur.

Narrator I nodded, bound to silence in the spell
of Hugh's ambition. Then our shadows fell
over a patch of bone-dry scree and – whizz –
up shot a cloud of blue fritillaries
like the Portland Vase burst into smithereens.
But Hugh stood staring straight into the West
as though some sudden revelation tore him
bodily into the sky from the Pennine crest.

Hugh It's music. It's Bach made visible.

Narrator I didn't nod
this time, but contradicted my hero:

Ronald It's not.
No, Hugh. You've got
the wrong metaphor. It's Turner. He's borrowed his palette from God
and is painting his sunset for him.

Hugh (*A bit nettled*) Who told you about Turner?

Ronald Robb. He was on about poets painting in words.
And artists seeing poetry in flying birds.

Hugh (*Laughing*) Then Robb mixed his metaphors.

Ronald He didn't. He says poets are the greatest artists of all.
They can see beauty where others can't. If they've got the call.
Hugh, have you heard of the *London Mercury*?

Hugh Of course. It's the leading literary rag.
Well – put it that way. A cut above the school mag.

Ronald Don't be an ass. Robb sent J. C. Squire, the editor,
a sample or two of my poetry.

Hugh (*In surprise*) To Squire? He isn't going to print it?

Ronald No.
He said it showed great promise.

And said he was sorry to have to give a dusty answer,
but if that didn't discourage me, then . . . one day . . .
(*Suddenly, flatly*) I'm going to be a poet.

Hugh Right. See that notice:
DON'T TIP RUBBISH IN THE GOIT.
Write a poem about that.

Ronald Very well. I will. If you promise not to show it to anyone.

Hugh Cross my heart and may I die.

Ronald You wait and see.

Narrator That, I think, was the moment of truth for me.
The point on which the whole of my real life turned.
With that absurd challenge, a gauntlet so easy to fling,
I somehow learned
the meaning – and the promise – of the warning,
those whose god is Mammon regard with scorning:

Voice 'Drink deep, or taste not the Pierian spring.'

Ronald I'm going to be a poet.

Narrator So the Easter term went by,
exciting, timeless, fleet
in the company of Hugh –
often, in class, with scarce a clue
on minute-dragging feet.
One morning, when Harrison took geography –
he of the caustic tongue, the sudden rap –
spiritual homesickness overpowered me
and so I drew
my beloved South Milford map.
Harrison's shafts:

Harrison May heaven keep me sane:
Rain, Miller, you stupid boy, convectional rain
is caused by air rising over a watershed . . .

Narrator – such arrows flew harmlessly above my head.
I drew, inaccurately, each field I knew
like the palms of my hands – each wood –
the stream where a solitary heron stood
one leg drawn up, isoceles-triangled
as, greyly patient, he angled.
I drew the village, the gasholder, the station . . .

Porter (*singing out*) South Milford!

Narrator South Milford. That's to say

the plainest, the most humdrum, the most everyday
of villages in creation.
Yet, to me then, as now, South Milford lies
in God's comprehensive view,
as Caxton sang: 'fore-to
the Gates of Paradise.'
Harrison touched my shoulder. He said:

Harrison Find out
which people put your village where it is – and when, and why
– that's what geography is really about.

Narrator My memory flashes from the words he spoke
to the clicked rhythm of the holiday train.
(*Fade up sleepy steam train*)
With sleepy huffs and chuffs of dragon smoke
it stopped at the country station, the loved, the plain
quintessence of the commonplace again.
(*Train stops. Slam open carriage door. Jump on to platform two pairs of feet*)

Neville Good old South Milford.

Narrator (*Luxurious sniff*) Creosote.

Neville (*More luxurious, longer sniff*) Melted tar.
Ron – Uncle Harold!

Ronald With a new Bean car!
Good lord!

Harold (*About 37, very attractive voice. Calling*)
Afternoon, Admiral. Look sharp and I'll pipe you aboard.
(*Spirited whistle. Car doors slam. Car starts*)

Neville Have you sold the old Day-Leeds, Uncle? Uncle, have you still got the gig and the trap
and Snowball and Judy? Does Buller still catch rats
in the loose boxes? Does . . .

Harold Here, hold hard, old chap.
I've still got the Day-Leeds. The hunters are out at grass.
But Judy's dead, and poor old Buller too.
That nearly broke Tom's heart. And mine. That do?

Neville Can we play tennis on the court in the paddock? And cricket?

Ronald (*In what he supposes to be a whisper*) Shut up, you ass.
You'd drive anybody bats.

Harold (*Laughing*) That's right. You sit on his head, Ron. Just the ticket.

Narrator Silence made Neville squirm

for as long as it takes a starling to gulp a worm.
Neville Uncle Harold, I'm going to school with Ron next term.
Narrator I should have been as overjoyed as he –
but Hugh, in one term, had widened the four-year gap
between my brother and me
to as far apart as the Vale of York on the map
from half-way up Mickle Fell.
Neville Ron: this is going to be the best holiday, ever, ever, ever.
Narrator I loved my brother well.
But he still whooped with the Red Indians on boyhood's plain
while I'd climbed the hills with Hugh.
Robb had half challenged, half tempted me to pursue
an austere dream of endeavour,
which stirred the more because part understood
like adolescence mantling my cheeks with blood.
Neville, immune as yet from the disease
endemic by one of nature's cruellest laws,
spotted its symptons with clear-sighted ease
and laid a jibing finger on the cause.
Neville (*Taunting*) You're sweet on Dorothy.
Ronald I'm not! I'm not!
Narrator The lad's love misery
of the green sickness, its magic-chance delights
as random as the fitful breeze which shook
five wild rose petals adrift along the brook
– as unexpected as the kingfisher's flight –
as scattered as corn-cockles in the wheat,
made all that summer headier than meadowsweet.
Neville (*Sings jeeringly*) 'Who were you with last night?
Out in the pale moonlight?
It wasn't your mother. It wasn't . . .'
Ronald (*Furiously*) I've a jolly good mind to give you a clip on the ear.
Neville I didn't see you kissing her in Plum Tree Lane. No fear.
Oh, didn't Ronnie Ward laugh when I told him.
Ronald I'll murder you.
Narrator Fools laugh at calf love, moony-eyed.
(*Laughing*) And moon calf ears, dyed crimson, make
fine targets for the comic spirit.
The village, like the family, smiled
to see me solemnly beguiled

like Bottom in his magic dream.
Villager He's gormless.
Neville (*Choking laughter*) Isn't Ron a scream?
Narrator My Uncle Harold understood
why I went wandering Milford lanes
enduring young love's teething pains.
My uncle, at whose feet I'd sat,
in kid boots and silk petticoats
when he married my father's elder sister
on a July day of nineteen-ten...
Harold H'm. The world was different then.
Narrator A doctor, he knew of antidotes
for rarer fevers of the blood
than the greensickness in the veins.
(*Pause*)
I felt the pull of Harold Radcliffe's mind –
a trifle lonely in its orbit, I think,
as he went the rounds of eleven out-surgeries
– a task to make the most dedicated blink –
from Barkston Ash to Hambleton, Burton Salmon, Brotherton,
Ledsham, Hillam, Micklefield,
black as the slack of its coal-seam's yield,
hot-hearted, poor as its miners' pay.
(*Fade up car*)
I went the rounds with him, day after day.
He had the knack
of keeping the thread of a conversation.
He'd stop to visit a back-to-back
for three minutes, maybe; maybe thirty,
then on to Sherburn, as clean and green
as Micklefield was mean and dirty.
Harold As I was saying, Ron, men's occupation
moulds 'em, when they work close to or under the earth –
but not in the same mould.
Look closely – no plough-seam's the same as the next fold.
'Morning, Jack.
Jack (*As they pass*) 'Morning, Doctor.
Harold The roadmender.
My father attended his mother at his birth.
Notice his monocle? It's got an iron rim.

It's not there for fancy: the sight in his good eye's dim.
Old Jack's a character.
He's proud of that monocle. Amuses him.
You'd never guess his hobby...

P.C. (*Singing out from bicycle*) Doctor....

Ronald A bobby.

Narrator His feet
pedalled more furiously as we slowed.

Harold (*Professional calm*) Accident?

P.C. (*Respectful professional officiousness*)
No, Doctor. Official inquiry. Did you meet
a red-bearded tramp proceeding on the Selby road?

Harold I did.

Narrator Satisfaction relaxed the official manner.

P.C. Did you give him owt?

Harold As a matter of fact, a tanner.

P.C. (*Increased satisfaction*) I'll make a note.
He's a known bad character.
'Looking for work'? They're workshy.
They're all over the country. You shouldn't encourage 'em, sir.

Harold (*Very wryly: he knows far more about tramps than the PC*)
Thanks for the tip.

Narrator On the way back, we saw the red-bearded one,
recumbent on one hip,
sharing the grass verge with the cabbage whites and the sun.

Harold Hi, you!

Narrator The flip
of the florin made a silver ripple to startle alike
the air and the tramp.

Harold No bobby on a bike
is going to deprive me of my valued membership
of the Royal and Antediluvian Order of Mugs.

Narrator He gave that smile of irony, which tugs
the corners of the mouth down, to deride
its own compassion, close-allied
to love, as in the physician, Luke.
In Harold, compassion could rebuke.
At Fairburn I waited for an hour outside
a miner's cottage, one up, one down, in a row
identical as pauper's coffins.

Woman Mug o' tea?
(*Apologetically*) It's nobbut condensed milk – but we've gotten nowt
i' Fairburn.
(*Confidentially*) Eh, Doctor's vexed wi' me.
He took one look at Em, us second daughter . . .

Harold (*Terse*) A basin. Your cleanest towel. Boiling water.
Get the neighbours out.

Woman By gow, he made 'em scat.
And then he laid t'bairn on t'table and slit her throat.

Harold Hold her down.

Woman First time ivver I've heard shout.
Then he put his lips tiv her throat and sucked and spat,
sucked and spat into t'basin, blood and yellow stuff.
(*Solicitously*) Nay, then, isn't tea sweet enough?

Harold She's over the worst. She can breathe.
Why didn't you call me sooner? Couldn't you see she was ill?

Woman (*Faltering*) Yes, Doctor. But us owed you . . .

Narrator I could almost feel his anger seethe.

Harold (*Extreme cold anger*) Burn the bill.
(*Harold starts the car violently*)
And burn the rogues who still refuse to lay the drains.

Narrator Ten minutes – and he was telling me that tramps still used the lanes
tramped by the Yorkist armies to Towton field.
Ten minutes more – and then September sealed
the eyes of dying summer with a kiss
and Neville was at Crossleys, in Form One
and school shorts, misery and the wriggling bliss
of the fighting shallows, darting with small fry,
where the well-timed fart was art and wit a pun.
School did not draw us closer. For why?
Our houses were of different tartans.
I was Trojans; Neville, Spartans.
On Sundays, by the school's long use
brothers under flag of truce
renewed their old and deep-set liking
– though one was Paladin, t'other Viking,
one brilliant in the lower school,
his senior a fifth-form fool.

On Sundays, what was I to do?
Hugh The moors, as usual?
Ronald Right-ho, Hugh.
Narrator In those long walks I learned
in silences between
our ranging talk
to see how a vein of green
in a brown stone upturned
blended subtly with the dead heather
and a grouse's blood-stained feather
and all three with the blue
of the mare's tail streaked sky
as colour matchers do.
So, now fast, now slow,
the autumn term went by.
(*Chorus to an accompaniment of banged desk lids*)
Chorus No more Latin, no more French,
no more sitting on a hard, cold bench.
(*Fade up steam train*)
Narrator Our snorting dragon homeward rolled,
its livery of green and gold
sheeted by the foothills-sleet.
(*Train slows at terminus*)
Porter Leeeeeeeds.
(*Cross-fade train to traffic*)
Narrator Out we rushed, on pounding feet,
to run and run to City Square.
Neville Good old Black Prince.
Narrator Discreetly bare
his nymphs exposed their dimpled knees.
The wind was cold enough to freeze
their bronze revealing draperies.
Neville Five days to Christmas. Oh, how glad I am
to be back in good old Leeds, in good old String-o'-Beads.
Quick, Ron – the Harehills tram.
Ronald Sprint. I'll lug your suitcase.
Neville There.
(*Single ping of tram bell. Tram moves off*)
Ronald Upstairs.
Narrator He swung his shorter feet

underneath the toast-rack seat.
Thus, close-perched, we swayed and lurched
to whining, droning ululation.
Huge hoardings everywhere
in colours as crude
as the Northern city, glared
under carbon arc lamps
so that when the wind swung
their shades, they flung
bat-wing shadows upon:

Voice (*These voices all shout*) Owbridge's lung tonic.

Voice Mother Seager's.

Voice Allenbury's food.

Neville Look, look, Ron:
Hardy's CHRISTMAS TOY FAIR.
Oh, I do hope Aunt Jess'll take us there.
(*Loud ping of tram bell*)

Conductor Briggate.

Neville Only nineteen more stops.

Narrator Neville, like the tram, droned on and on,
waxed shrill at a picture house,
went ping over lighted shops.
I didn't hear him. My mind was with Moby Dick
and the mad captain with his ivory stump:

Ahab There she blows!

Narrator It wasn't Ahab's yell that made me jump
but Neville's:

Neville You make me sick.

Narrator He was crimson to the tip of his nose.

Neville You haven't listened to a word I've said.
You never do.
You only talk about beastly books you've read.
Books. That's what you talk about to mouldy old Moles.
Know what Pip Musther calls him?

Pip (*Same age as Neville: jeering parody of Hugh's voice*)
Ikey Boles.

Neville Pip's got a real brother, Pip has. Coo –
and I looked forward to going to school with you.

Ronald Oh, Neville...

Neville Take your arm away. You're a pig.

Narrator He flicked a sideways tongue to lick a tear
and gulped. He'd got the wrong word by the ear:
I knew the word he should have used was 'prig'..
That night in bed, his head
lay cradled by my arm
and we talked, as we used to talk at Low Moor Farm
until the sheets grew warm and he fell asleep.
But the Great Bear's tail and the Little Bear's tail
seemed to be trapped by the skylight-frame
and between them, yellow-pale,
I could see Arcturus, the Bearward's flame
deep in the forest of the night
where Blake's tyger, burning-bright,
prowled in that utter loneliness
man knows in his inmost heart –
a wilderness
which is beyond, yet in our ken,
a wilderness which keeps all men
both together and apart.
I felt on my cheek my brother's breath.
He, my brother,
was as close to me as death
which had taken our father and our mother.
And death's brother, Morpheus,
who sometimes helps death to reap,
smiled, half sad, half humorous
and carried me into the Cave of Sleep.
(*Pause*)
Next night we larked about and Neville, growing sillier,
threw one of his boots at me and so brought down
an alcove curtain.
(*A boot is thrown and the curtain comes down*)

Neville Ron. Come here.

Narrator There were five stone bottles, portly as abbots, brown
as Carmelite monks.

Both Harry Holgate's gingerbeer!

Narrator Treasure trove, as exciting, as inviting
our fingers to try the rimmed tops, screwed down tight –
until by the blue gaslight
I read on the labels my grandmother's crab-apple writing.

Grandmother Cowslip. Hawthorn Blossom. Raspberry Vinegar 1920.
Neville (*Disgusted*) So that's why grandma filled us up with pop.
Grandmother Dandelion . . . Parsnip
Narrator We gazed, appalled.
Neville (*Disgusted*) What a sell. (*Resigned*) C'mon. Turn in.
Ronald (*Bright practical idea*)
Let's not undress. It's going to freeze.
Neville Good idea. Righty-ho.
(*They scramble into bed*)
(*Brooding*) Dandelion. Dandelion.
Ronald Nev: d'you know?
That's my name for Great-aunt Jin.
I like her. She's sort of warm and sunny.
Neville (*Catching on, gurgles*) Great-aunt Suff's Parsnip.
Aren't they funny?
Narrator Soon, with one unerring leap
out of darkness, shadow-hung,
silently the cat of sleep
caught the red mouse of his tongue.
(*Pause*)
Maybe my fingers had loosened a bottle top
for in the holy middle of the night
it blew up . . .
(*Shattering explosion*)
like a depth charge dropped on a submarine.
(*Depth charge*)
And as a smithereen
fell on the bed between us . . .
(*Third depth charge*)
up went the third.
The ceiling splashed and dripped
with home-made wine.
Dandelion and Parsnip
creamed, foamed and gurgled.
Jess, with a candle, opened the attic door.
Jess Good heavens!
Narrator The wavering candlelight blurred.
We crept to the stairhead.
We saw the flood cascading
with uncertain pour,

foaming and frothing, pink staining gold, gold, green.
And then Jess, shading
her candle, saw us –
save for our collars and boots
fully, if crumply clothed And helpless hoots
of wrath and laughter made her turn as pink
as the wine, going down like suds in a kitchen sink.
And need I say
my grandmother took it in her own sweet way:

Grandmother Bless me.
(*Grandmother clock ticks*)

Narrator My grandmother's clock was as short as herself
and its voice matched her resonant voice.

Grandmother As bright was its face
as my best kitchen Delft
and the satiny sheen of its fine walnut case
made the strings of my old heart rejoice.

Narrator Its well-commanded, bell-commanded
timing, chiming voice fell dumb
full four decades ago.
Like her heart, its pendulum
came to equilibrium
between imperatives of To,
imperatives of Fro.
(*Clock tick stops*)

Jess Mother...

Narrator The grief of Jess was gentle, if intense,
for death had entered the house with deference
and no peremptory knock.
Before the funeral
the eventual silence of the unwound clock
must have let fall
an in memoriam shock,
and afterwards made bolder still the mouse
left the sole tenant of the empty house.

Summer with Flowers that Fell

Summer With Flowers That Fell was first broadcast on BBC Radio 4 on 6 August 1972 with the following cast:

NARRATOR	*Stephen Murray*
RONALD SCRIVEN	*Judy Bennett*
MATRON	*Kathleen Helme*
NEVILLE SCRIVEN	*Jo Manning Wilson*
UNCLE HAROLD	*William Eedle*
MRS. RYDER	*Katherine Parr*
TED RYDER	*Robin Browne*
ROSE	*Helen Worth*

Produced by Charles Lefeaux

(*Music – 'A Song of Summer' by Delius*)

Narrator All early in the April night
of my forebeing,
separate, but not apart,
my heart beat . . .
(*Child's heartbeat, 144 a minute*)
under my mother's heart . . .
(*Beat of adult heart, 72 a minute*)
unbreathing, unseeing.
An hour after dawn, next day
I crossed two barriers which lay
between me and eventual death.
My sight took the sundering shock of light:
my lungs, the separating gulp of breath.
(*Baby's birth-wall*)
So all men born of a woman are born to pain and delight.
(*Music – 'Irmelin' by Delius*)
A little farther on the way,
through lands I'd partly learned to map,
or seas I'd partly learned to chart,
I, separate, unique, apart,
thought myself a likely chap:
I was gawky, headstrong, salad-green,
ambition's feather in my cap.
The song in my heart was short and gay
clean as the winds of March are clean.

Ronald Oh, roll on April. Come the day
when I shall be fifteen!

Narrator I thought I'd learned so much, so much
from sight, smell, hearing, taste and touch,
and yet my innocence was such
I had not grasped the labyrinth's clue:
that brain and sinew, bone and flesh,
closely though they intermesh
are not an integrated whole,
save in moments rare and few,
instants never ours to choose,
when, fleetingly, wing-beatingly,

between the earth and sky, they fuse
rapturously, with the soul.
This, I half-knew, instinctively.
Romantic poets I prized above
all others, jostled to agree
that I would know such ecstasy
when I first really fell in love.
No June-rose girl, no rainbow-arch,
no dragon's-blood-dyed sunset sea
cloud-magicked out of Hy Brasil,
thus suddenly, enchanted me –
(*Fade up school rugger match and a cold wind*)
but the smack of a greasy rugger pill
on a school playing field that March
of mud and sleet and pewter skies.
(*Thud of rugger-ball – Suggest punch-ball*)
The pass, high slung by Fox from Young,
had the sharp impact of surprise.
(*Ref's whistle*)
The house match, dribble, kick and hack,
hard-pressed defence and foiled attack,
up to half-time had brought no score.
Ten minutes from time, the Spartan pack
had driven us into our twenty-five
and the ball was mine. Just being alive
was joy divine.
(*Ref's whistle,*)

Ref (*In distance*) Forward pass.

Narrator The ball was mine,
I had not heard
the whistle. Everything suddenly blurred,
together. Our Viking war-whoop rose:

All Ahoy!

Narrator I thought:

Ronald (*Exultant*) I'll show them now. Here goes.

Narrator Watchful, arms akimbo, stood
the Spartan full back, Umpleby.
I gulped in air. It smelled of mud,
leather, sleet, dead winter grass.
Two Spartan forwards in front of me – three.

Above the goalposts' arms, upflung
to prop the tarnished pewter sky,
I saw a crack,
a glint of sun.
And suddenly
mud, sky, grass and sleet were one
with pulsing blood and rib-tight lung,
one glorious whole,
mind, body and soul
in ecstatic union.
I dodged, swerved, and began to run.
(*Distant ref's long-drawn whistle. Mocking cheer*)
The Spartan, not my Trojan hosts
derisively
cheered the try
I thought I'd scored between the posts.
(*Longer distant whistle*)
Willie Fox shouted:

Fox Scriven, you ass,
I know you're deaf,
but gosh, you must have heard the ref
whistling for a forward pass?

Ronald (*Mortified, indignant*) Was it heck!
Who slung it? You?

Fox (*Laughing*) I know. And you were behind me. True.
But truth is what the referee sees,
and when old Harrison referees
the voice of the ref is the will of God.

Narrator Ichabod.
The glory had indeed departed.
I slouched back, hating all humanity.
There was no balm in Gilead, none
to heal my wounded schoolboy vanity.
The caustic Trojan comments smarted
until the final whistle blew.
(*Long final whistle*)

Ref (*Brisk, schoolmasterly authority*)
Match drawn. Replay next week. Come on.

Narrator Then, in 1922,
our playing field had no pavilion:

the school believed in hardihood.
So, in a streaming, foxhound flood –
lemon-and-dash, liver-and-tan –
both packs intermingling, ran
the long uphill mile back to school.
Downcast, loitering, I lagged behind,
heedless that the moorland wind
rapidly began to cool
my sweaty shirt, chest-caked with mud.

Fox (*Calling back*) Buck up!

Narrator I could be led:
I wouldn't be driven.
First, deliberately, I slowed
to a walking pace, then left the road.
Grassland, part public park, part moor,
rough going, tussocky and choppy
led to the school, majestical,
dating to 1764,
all grey stone. A vile, Victorian copy
of its proud original,
a palace on the Grand Canal.
On a weathered wooden bench
just outside the school's main gate
stood a seedy reprobate
who sought to clench
conviction with spasmodic jerks
of bony arms, tossed anyhow.
His discourse seemed to fascinate
two nursemaids and five out-of-works.

Sinner (*Gloating over past iniquity*)
I was a sinner of the blackest dye.
(*Abrupt descent to matter-of-fact*) But I'm not now.

Voice (*Equally matter-of-fact*) Liar.

Sinner (*Indignation, modified by touch of regret*)
I'm not. I'll tell you how it came to pass.
(*Propounding logical argument*)
Sitha. As true as I'm standing on this here seat,
I was saved from hellfire by a Salvation Army lass
two years ago last on Good Friday,
in the Old Cock public house in Silver Street.

She took a pint from me hand and shouted:
(*Quick fade up of noisy pub*)

Lass Sinner, repent.

Sinner Scales dropped from me eyes as they dropped from Saul's on t' Damascus Road.
(*Dramatically*) I looked in her bonny blue e'en. By gow, they glowed.

Lass (*Fervent, pleading*) Sinner, draw back from the edge
of Satan's pit of fire and brimstone. Come,
be washed in the blood of the Lamb.
(*Fade pub*)

Sinner And so, by damn,
I went to the Town Hall Square and signed the pledge
there and then, while she steadied me hand on the big bass drum.

Voice (*Healthy scepticism*) Then tha wert letting on.
Tha'd gotten a right skinful when I see'd thi last neet,
in t' four-ale bar of t' owd White Swan.
(*A burst of laughter from two nursemaids and five down-and-outs*)

Narrator A flurry of snow dispersed his audience
and sent me scurrying along the path
and by a side door to the school gymnasium.
The others had tubbed and scrubbed, and changed and gone.
I stripped and wallowed, submerged to my chin in the bath.
Drying myself, I shivered suddenly.
In hall, I had no appetite for tea;
I trailed the corridor with listless step.
(*The school bell*)
Then the bell went for prep.

Ronald (*Heavy sigh, dragged sentences*) On the poetry ... of ... Blake.
Poor Robb.
Yes ... should be just ... the job.
(*The pages of a book are ruffled*)
Robb said ...
But where are my notes? Ah, here ...
Blake was a p-p-poet's poet.
That is a seer ...
(*Rasping breath*) His sight made clear by inward light.
What example should I take?

Narrator I gave my lips a furtive lick

shuddered, and felt icy sick.

Ronald 'Tyger, Tyger, burning b-bright
In the forests . . . of the night . . .'
I feel rotten . . .
Can't get on with the b-beastly thing.

Master (*Abruptly*) What's up, Scriven?
You're looking white.

Ronald (*Teeth chattering*) Dunno sir.

Master You're shivering.
(*Decisively*) Better see Matron.

Narrator Miss Wilkinson
felt my forehead. Her hand seemed iced.
She had that kind of cool, brisk poise,
cross-card indiced,
with laundry bills, and tradesmen's bills,
and a wide conspectus of all the ills
real or imaginary, of boys.
Her hand on my forehead, her glance sufficed.
She shook down her thermometer,
and said:

Matron (*No accent*) Into the sick bay and straight to bed.

Narrator Where the sheets touched me, they were clammy
as churchyard mould.
Why was my flesh as hot as they were cold?
Why did my icy temples throb and ache
while through my head there ran,
not the magnificent tyger forged by Blake,
but lines of Flecker's which jigged like sand-devils, spun
tormentingly, beneath the desert sun.

Ronald (*Feverishly*) 'The sun, who flashes through the head
and paints the shadows green and red,
The Sun shall eat thy fleshless dead, O Caravan, O Caravan!'
(*Characteristic pneumonia cough*)

Narrator I coughed. From my ribs a green-red pain
leaped through my nerves to kick my brain.
My sight blurred, cleared, and at my side
a vague, white shadow solidified.

Ronald (*With difficulty, but confidently*)
Please, nurse, may I have a drink of water?

Nurse (*Not unkindly, but firmly*) No. Doctor's orders.

Narrator She was professional, matter of fact.
Ronald (*Pleading*) Please, please. My throat's burning. Please, nurse.
I think I shall die
unless I have a glass of water to drink.
Nurse No. You've got pneumonia. The doctor says
that even one drink of water would make it worse.
Narrator That was the nightmare's beginning. Nights and days
telescoped into, and then out of, each other,
like images of water sliding over the brink
of Niagara into Sahara sands, bleach-dry.
Then, in a mirage of delirium, Neville, my brother,
appeared and said:
Neville (*About ten. Impressed by what he's been told*)
Hello. Are you feeling any better, Ron?
Ronald Put your hand on my forehead.
Neville Gosh.
Ronald (*Teeth chatter*) Don't snatch it away. It's icy. You can't possibly be a sand-devil
Neville 'Course not, Ron. You must be ill. It's me, Neville.
Ronald (*Imperative, elder to younger brother*)
Get me some water, quick.
Neville (*Self-defensive*) I couldn't, when you asked me yesterday.
Ronald (*Very positive*) I didn't.
Narrator Neville seemed to disappear
then reappear, like a rabbit in a conjuring trick.
Neville I did. Don't you remember? Sister sent me away.
She said you weren't right in your head.
I've got something better. A bottle of ginger beer.
It's under my waistcoat.
Ronald Give it here. Wow!
Nurse is coming.
Narrator Neville fled.
That bottle of pop, gulped surreptitiously,
cooled all my being, as deliciously
as though I were Dives tormented in hell's flame.
That night, the crisis came.
The ceiling of the small sick-bay was white,
the walls were painted flat-white, epicene,
white candlewick bedspreads breathed: Hygiene.
White curtains shaded the windows from the light

which made my eyes ache in the rectangular cell,
where, not knowing day from night,
I lay, hot-shivering, in my Arctic hell.
In the quietude
of what I wrongly thought was solitude,
I suddenly heard a small, still voice, ice-clear:

Pain You know me. I am pain.
I drove a red-hot screw into your ear
slowly . . . remember? . . . like this . . .

Narrator I made a rasping noise. I could not hiss
because of the swollen soreness of my tongue.

Pain I pierced one ear-drum, but I was merciful
and was content to make the other dull.

Narrator I tried to scream –
(*A strangulated noise*)
in vain.
I was back, in delirium, in my childhood home again.
I lay on the sofa
in a room coloured red by my bloodshot eyes.
I heard the voice of my brother:

Neville (*Aged four*) Don't cry, Ron.

Narrator An actual sound croaked from me:

Ronald Mother, Mother.

Pain Your mother is dead. Your father is dead.
Had you forgotten?
It was memory, not I, tightening the screw in your ear.
Now I shall tighten the bands of pleurisy about your lungs
as a torturer tightens the rack.
Your throat shall throb like the bite of serpent-tongues.
Your ribs shall crack.

Narrator A shadow moved over me, amorphous, tall.
I turned my face to the wall. (*Long pause*)
(*Change tone to one of detached observation*)
There was a hair-line crack, diagonal, faint,
in the wall's flat-white paint.
It widened, like a pair of monstrous lips.
Out of it, as I stared, terrified, obtuse,
a thing, like a huge, blind slug began to ooze.
I knew it had come to kill pain.
I smelt the sick-room smell

which was its breath.
A voice, far-off, pierced the cold mist of my brain:
Matron (*Firm, steady, Nonconformist*)
There's only one thing now: prayer. (*Long pause*)
(*Direct, the strong voice of old-fashioned faith*)
As Jacob wrestled with another angel,
Lord, give me strength to wrestle with the angel of death.
(*Long pause. Confident composure*) There.
Narrator The looming shadow stooped closer, and
closed on my shoulder with iron fingertips:
Matron Ronald:
turn your face away from the wall.
Narrator Even on that threshold, I knew the voice of command.
Matron You are very ill. You are not going to die.
I will not let you die.
Do you understand?
Narrator I think I babbled incoherently
wandering far out of my mind,
as the hands of love sought, and fought, agonisingly
as my body felt, to unbind
the ligatures of fever, tightening yet.
Her hands, again and again
cleansed away the poisonous, oozing sweat
and cooled the fever-fret,
relaxing, fraction by fraction, the grip of pain.
Through the small hours, those hands fought on my side,
in the battle all mortal flesh must wage, for breath.
Wearied out, in the false dawn, she saw me glide
and drift away upon the turning tide
which carries so many out to the uttermost deep.
I was borne, on that tide, not to the cave of death
but of his brother, sleep.
(*Music: 'Irmelin' by Delius*)
(*Fade up dawn chorus of binds*)
All early in the April
lark, blackbird, linnet, thrush,
the sparrow from the rooftop,
the wren from the lilac bush,
began their joyous chorus
adoring dawn's first blush.

The sun, stirred by their ecstasies,
drew across my eyelashes
a quivering, iris brush.
I heard thrush, linnet, blackbird sing
with the lark, on heaven's blue wing:
(*There is a burst of each bird's song under its words*)

Thrush The earth is green...

Linnet ... is green again.

Blackbird For April sun, so goldenkind,
for April rain on the warm west wind...

Lark ... thanks be to God.

All For being alive...

Lark ... thanks be to God, thanks be to God.

Narrator I raised my head from the pillow,
I saw the sky, the trees,
I saw the curtains billow,
I felt the warm-cool breeze
and all my being was dizzy with bliss for all of these.

Nurse You're not to get up. You know what the doctor said.
Your brother Neville has come to say goodbye to you.

Neville (*Extremely cheerful*) Still in bed?
I've not much time. Any messages to send?

Ronald One or two.

Neville We've all been bunging our suitcases down the staircase-well from the dorm.

Ronald How have the exams gone?

Neville All right. Next term, I go up to the third form.

Ronald Good. Wish I were going home with you.
I'll miss a week of the hols at least.

Neville (*Laconic fraternal sympathy*) Rotten luck.

Ronald Miss Wilkinson's staying to look after me. She's a beast.

Neville A pill!

Ronald She bullied me when I was really ill.
(*Grudgingly*) She's been a bit better since.

Nurse (*Calling from door*) Come on.

Neville Bother!

Nurse Neville.

Neville I've got to scoot now. Goodbye, Ron.

Narrator To my beloved South Milford, my village of heart's ease,
I returned with daylight's random stars, the first pale primroses.

Excitement's effervescence
frothed the bloodstream in my veins.
Then listlessness and convalescence,
limp of spine,
linked their languid arms with mine
as I strolled through country lanes.
My fifteenth birthday, longed for so ardently,
was rather a damp squib.
My Uncle Harold raised his brows to me:

Harold Well, Colonel?

Narrator The corners of his lips gave a down-tugged tweak
of humorously gentle irony.
I smiled at him – and the familiar jest.

Harold Suppose you and I step into the surgery?

Narrator I lay on the prickly, black horsehair settee –
his father's long ago:

Harold I'll run the stethsocope over your back and chest.
M'mm.
(*Dissatisfied*) M'mm (*Pause*)
You need a change of air –
and scenery.
It's clear that Milford hasn't done the trick.
I'll send you to Masham. You have relations there.
(*It's pronounced – Mass'm*)

Ronald (*Immediate interest*) Where's Masham? Oh, uncle, you are a brick.

Harold Masham's in Wensleydale. It'll give you what you need,
a complete change, my boy – and that's the essence,
psychologically, to carry you through convalescence.
But remember: more haste, less speed.
No long walks at first.

Ronald I don't want to go for walks. I'll read
and read and read. Nothing but poetry.
Rupert Brooke. Flecker. The Golden Treasury.
I've got them here. Please, may I borrow Herrick
and Keats and Shelley?

Harold (*Teasing*) Yes. Are you sure you wouldn't rather take Eric
or Little by Little? Or Nat the Naturalist?

Ronald No.

Harold Take Herrick, Keats and Shelley. But bring them back.

Narrator I flung them gaily into a haversack.

(*Fade up 1922 car in motion*)
Tom drove me to Masham on St George's Day
through steep dales country, gay
with April's first, most lyric greenery.
Tom, my uncle's groom-chauffeur-handyman,
ironic, laconic, from the moment our journey began
had little to say on the winding, rising way –
I, less – but I used my eyes.
At last we topped the crest of the last rise.
There, on surmise,
Tom, pushing back his peaked cap, set the seal
of certainty, in one word:

Tom Masham.

Narrator Like a cup, ill-shaped on the wheel
by the hand of a 'prentice potter
from a lump of wobbly clay –
and yet serene,
because he had the feel,
the love of his craft –
the valley of Masham lay.
I think his master laughed,
saying:

Master (*Hearty laugh*) Nay, lad, nay.

Narrator . . . then fired it, in the furnace, glazed with a sheen,
a bloom, of soft, grass green.
The walls of the cup, uneven from ridge to ridge,
sloped down to a hump-backed bridge,
a little out of plumb,
the mark, as it were, left by that 'prentice thumb.

Ronald What's the name of the river, Tom?

Tom The Ure.

Narrator We took the bridge with a slight, heart-starting lift.
Between water meadows, sparkling light, at war
with sparkling water, made the air change and shift
about two runners, crossing in mid-wicket.
Tom slowed the car a moment:

Tom Just the ticket.

(*Pause*)

Umpire (*A shout in the distance*) Not out.

Narrator Tom drove on up the hill to a cobbled square

and the gate of a small, trim house with a garden of soft fruit
bushes,
two apple trees and a pear.
A small, trim woman opened the gate:

Mrs Ryder (*About 40. Warm voice, a bit countrified, educated*)
Well, there.

Narrator Like Alfred Jingle, she talked in quickfire rushes
of twenty to the dozen.

Mrs Ryder Let me look at you. You won't remember me.
It's ages since I nursed you on my knee.
You're not like your father. Poor Jack. My quarter cousin.
You can call me Aunt Kitty.
My boy's nineteen. He's almost a man, my Ted.

Narrator She kissed me, suddenly.

Mrs Ryder His father's dead.
The war.

Narrator Like her long print dress,
she was faded and pretty
and her hand was as clean and hard as a rolling-pin.

Mrs Ryder They say I've a likeness to your dear Aunt Jess.
But what am I thinking of? Come in, come in.

Narrator I thought I'd be there for, at most, a week or two.

Ronald I might get a bit of cricket, Tom,

Narrator I said
when we shook hands.

Tom There'll be no cricket for you
I reckon, this side o' July.

Ronald Oh, well, at school.

Tom You're not going back till after the summer term.
Your uncle's orders.
Look after yourself, Ron. Goodbye.

Narrator I began to feel less mentally like a worm
and physically like a weed, as the days went by.
Hardy weather 'the cuckoo likes,
when showers betumble the chestnut spikes'
lured me farther out and about
to watch the water-ringed, rising trout
greedily feed,
by the watermill
under the steeple-crested hill,

on June's greenfly.

Ronald Fish (fly-replete in depth of June,
dawdling away their watery noon).

Narrator As a silver grayling took
the small, red earthworm wriggling, from my hook,
I murmured lovingly, the lovelier lines of Brooke.
Ted Ryder had given me a greenheart rod.
He'd promised to teach me how to tie a fly.
Ted was a fisherman born.
Ted, my new idol, whom I'd laughed to scorn
because he still read comics at nineteen,
Ted, who in a month had taught me more
of country lore
than I'd learned for myself in two years at Low Moor Farm
under the tyranny of Iron Ann.
(*Pause*)
Now, as though under an enchanter's nightshade charm
cross-rippling, lisping, time and the river ran
as idly as the poetry in my head.
I did not notice, in my drifting dream,
orange float dip on the darkening stream,
and was more startled when a quiet voice said:

Bailiff You'd catch more fish downstream of the water-wheel.

Ronald Ted told me to try my luck near the mill, Mr Peel.

Bailiff I'll show you the right spot, young'un.
(*Dog growls*)
Sally: heel.

Narrator The water bailiff knew I had a ticket.
He knew I was greener than Ted's greenheart rod
and left me, grinning, between the wheel and the weir.

Bailiff See those dippers? They know the water's fresher here –
churned up by the paddles. It'll be fresher, come the rain.

Narrator He went off with his basset. He looked like a Rural Dean,
fresh-faced, thickset, in homespun and brown gaiters.
I baited, cast and watched the float nid-nod.
The undershot wheel turned slowly . . . swish . . . swish . . . swish.
Little dippers, small, black, white-shirted head waiters,
bobbed on dry stones in midstream, dipped, bobbed again,
and still I caught no fish.
The banks, the river, the mill, the world smelled green.

Green, green and warm –
and down came the first heavy drops of a summer storm.
(Far rumble of thunder and rain)
I was soaked before I reached the nearest tree.
Looking back half a century,
idea, object, image, I see
interplay and live, all three,
resolve, dissolve, evolve – to be
incarnate in the drowning tree.
Not Niobe
had she wept slow grief for years
could weep such sad, unsalted tears.
Here the rain
with insane
god-like frenzy, absolutely
took his wooden Danae,
struck and stroked, direct, oblique,
now slackening its silver fury,
now tightening its mesh again.
Beauty, her body half awry,
leaned in dryad ecstasy
between the river and the sky.
(Fade rain)
At last, the rain god withdrew
and I,
wet through and through,
rejoiced, as all God's creatures, one by one,
rejoiced in the resurgence of the sun.
High and still higher in the ambient blue
the swallows, leaving the river reaches, flew.
Those swallows, which
I had watched, adroitly sewing, stitch by stitch
through sweet May weeks,
between the air and their fledglings' gaping beaks,
the threads, fine-spun
by hunger. And hunger drew,
with a coarser thread and half against my will,
my sun-soaked body, at last, up Masham Hill.

Mrs Ryder Oh, there you are. Wherever have you been?
High tea's on the table. Ted's raring to set to.

Ted (*Rougher voice than Kitty's*) Come on, man.
Ronald All serene.
Narrator In the scullery in haste
and cold, hard water, I washed.
Ted It's a real fine do.
Narrator He who does not know the taste
of Kitty Ryder's apple pie,
flakily crusted, criss-cross laced
by Wensleydale cream,
with, on the side, a chunky slice
cut from a round of Wensleydale cheese,
doesn't know of what saints dream,
diassatisfied with paradise.
Mrs Ryder A second helping, anyone?
Ted Aye.
Narrator Good manners went by the board:
Ronald Yes, please.
Mrs Ryder I'm glad you've found your appetite.
Ted Get it shifted. We're going out.
Mrs Ryder (*Warningly*) Ted.
Ted Yes, Mother. I know. Early to bed.
(*Chair pushed back: loud kiss*)
Nay, the things you worry about.
Come on, Ron.
(*Conspiratorially*) It's dark o' the moon tonight.
Narrator My senses were a-quiver.
(*Fade up quiet river and night atmosphere*)
In the dusk, all wood-smoke blue,
Ted made for the line of the river
as eels and otters do.
The honeysuckled smell of new-mown hay
was blent with warm earth and moisty river smells,
deepening night's ancestral mystery.
Ted (*Sharply*) Walk quietly.
Narrator I knew that Ted could hear
such sounds as the distant striking of church bells,
distinguish water chattering over stones
from the quick-sliding demi-semi-tones
of the mill race –
and place

the bark of a vixen half a mile away.

Ted What wind there is doesn't know which way to blow.
We leave the river here.
(*Fade river*)

Narrator In the owl-light, cat-a-prowl light,
we reached the edge of a wood,
drawn down like a close, dark hood
pulled over the brow of the hill.

Ted Don't breathe so loudly.
(*The sharp crack of a twig*)
Keep still.

Narrator Ted knelt in the dew-wet grass –
(*A match is struck*)
and struck a match and lit three candle stubs
in a poacher's lantern, made from a cocoa tin
and a bull's-eye burning glass.
He muffled the soft light with his handkerchief.

Ted Brock's about somewhere. I can smell him. He's teaching his cubs
how to hunt hedgehogs.
He and his missus have brought 'em up on grubs.
Hotchiwitchie. Romany for hedge-pig. That's what he likes.

Ronald Hedgehogs? What about the spikes?
A dog can't unroll them, once they're curled in a ball.

Ted Nor does an old badger. He munches 'em, spikes an' all.
Sh!
(*A badger approaches*)

Narrator I froze to a halt.
In the soft beam of the poacher's lantern I saw
an animal lurching like a half-drunk sailor.
His coat of pepper-and-salt
was rough, ill-cut, like the work of a country tailor.
He waddled towards me, working his underslung jaw.
I started, fascinated, at the first I'd met of his kind.

Ronald (*Whisper*) Isn't he scared of us?

Ted He's to windward – and almost blind.

Narrator Brock shambled until he came to the toe of my shoe.
At the smell of boot-polish he backed and grunted –
(*The badger grunts*)
a fine old English gentleman, deeply affronted.
From the moonless woodland ride a voice said:

Keeper (*Unaggressive satisfaction*) Well – nabbed you red-handed, eh, Ted?
Ted (*Startled: aggressive*) Have you hell.
Keeper (*Hardening*) Let's have a look at that lantern.
Narrator This fool rushed in
where poachers fear to tread.
Ronald (*Indignantly*) Ted wasn't after game.
He made that lantern in order to show me a badger.
Keeper Did he, my young cock spadger?
I thought it was one of his mother's birthday presents.
H'm! What you might call ingenious. Just the job
for spotting roosting pheasants.
What in your pockets? Partridge nets? Raisins soaked in whisky
and strung on a black hair plucked from a horse's tail?
Ah, guaranteed to stop a pheasant's gob.
Ted (*Sullen*) I wouldn't touch one in the nesting season.
Keeper Aye? You wouldn't rob a meadow pippit, I'll go bail.
Stands to reason,
the game's not worth the candle. Far too risky.
The bench comes down on it, savage. Chuck it, Ted,
for your mother's sake. Clear out, and go to bed.
Narrator The keeper kept the lantern. Mortified,
Ted used his tongue to lick his wounded pride.
But nearing home, he said:
Ted Long Sam was a pal of my dad.
My mother is as thick as thieves with his wife.
(*Beginning to laugh*) If Sam knew I'd never poached even a hare
in my life,
let alone a partridge, oh, wouldn't he be mad?
(*Peals of laughter from both boys*)
Narrator As the days lengthened
my body strengthened
like a colt's with the sun astride.
Muscle, sinew and nerve, increasingly
craving for action, dug their spurs in me.
Voice Stop idling...
Voice Stop dreaming...
Voice Action, action...
Narrator Their voices cried...
All Look. Cricket's playing along the river side.
Narrator The rough-cut grass, sprigged with daisies and red clovers

was a stage – with a glad green wood for backcloth – set
for a rustic minuet,
the pas-de-deux of the batsmen, the changing of overs,
the deliberate pas seul of the slow spin bowler.
(*Klok of batsman blocking ball*)

Voice (*Loud, confident*) Howzat?

Umpire (*Solemn after due pondering*) Not out.

Narrator Oh, to join this corps-de-ballet!
I saw the breaking of the last-wicket rally,
watched square-leg umpire ritually doff
five caps – and rushed to lend a hand with the roller.
The skipper, with honest warmth, said:

Skipper Bugger off!

Ronald If I can't play for the second, could I play for a scratch eleven?
I've played with the first, in South Milford. Well, only once.
But I was not out, seven!

Skipper (*As one mentioning Timbuctoo*) South Milford?

Narrator Contemptuous eyes stared at me over a chasm:

Skipper We want no bloody foreigners i' Masham.

Narrator On the rugger field, my pride had been castrated.
This hand-off irritated,
but didn't mortify.

Rose (*Country girl, not rough spoken, about 14*)
That's no reason to be a pig to him!

Narrator I heard a girl's voice cry. (*Pause*)
I looked at her, aglow.
Women are kittle cattle, creatures of mood and whim.
They take strange fancies to strangers – a fact I didn't know
being mixed up with reality,
sex, ideals and poetry
so long ago.
The girl had tumbled chestnut hair,
with here and there,
quick firefly glints.
Hazel eyes, with subtle hints
of green. Oh, candid-clear they were.
I was too shy to speak to her.
She might have been about fourteen.
She had the lure of the unknown.
I liked her looks – half understood

the village boys' hostility,
cold-shouldering me to Coventry.
Try to talk to her? What was the good?
Rejected by a village not my own,
downcast, not outcast, I wandered off alone.
I found some friends among the older folk.
Old Arthur, the wheelwright, tolerated me.
I was fascinated by his ancient craft.
He told me why gigs should have a lancewood shaft.

Arthur (*Deep, slowish voice*)
Lancewood. Fit for a king of the realm.
It's grand to work with wood, once you've gotten the feel.

Narrator He worked away in the shade as he made a wheel.

Arthur For the hub, elm.
Oak for the spoke,
ash for a felloe.

Narrator Stroke on stroke
old Arthur's chisel plied – his mall
thudded, to make chips scatter and fall.

Arthur Elm for the hub – like this, tha sees,
matured like a right good Wensleydale cheese.

Narrator He carved each oak spoke
close-grained, pale yellow.

Arthur Ash for the felloes. Ash, when green
is fire for a queen.
Ash, old,
is fire for a queen with a crown of gold.

Narrator Elm and oak, close-grained
cut by hand were shaped, bored, planed.
When the new-built wheel ran true
he shod it with an iron shoe,
heated, hammered, levered, wrenched
sledged and tapped and –
(*Sudden sizzle and hiss of hot metal in water*)
water-quenched.

Ronald (*Enthusiasm*) She's a beauty, Mr Todd.

Narrator Old Arthur gave a wink, a nod:

Arthur Five things a wheelwright can rely on.
Oak, elm, ash and iron –
and, as long as cold clenches and heat expands,

the skill built into his two hands.
Narrator Sawdust in the welt of either shoe,
the stubble on his chin a shadowy blue,
he knocked off for his pint in the tap of the Bear.
I loitered where the river loitered, through
the water-meadows, with as little care,
while the floating voice called from the wood:
Cuckoo (*Human voice*) Cuckoo.
Narrator In June the cuckoo changed his tune
and seemed to say:
Cuckoo Cu-uckoo. A swarm of bees in May
is worth a load of hay.
Cu-uck-OO.
A swarm of bees in June
is worth a silver spoon.
Narrator Pollen began to tickle
as the new moon sharpened her sickle
towards Midsummer Day.
The sun grew hotter.
Deep and still
ran the leat of the water mill.
Face down on the bank, I watched the stream,
myself a part of its summer dream.
Like thoughts one struggles to express
in the stream of consciousness,
brown trout let me see their scales,
then vanished, flickering their tails.
I had idled in water-meadows, as Anon
had loitered many a day in sparser acres.
Anon, High Master of the Order of the Makers,
Anon, who in the hills
drank from the springs and rills
of English verse.
Anon, who named the stars, each firefly spark,
and plucked a flower and called it:
Anon Shepherd's purse.
Narrator Under a willow, as I watched the water glide,
the Golden Treasury, green-cool by my side,
there mingled with water-music in my head
changing at the current's whim,

the voices of poets who had stemmed from him.
Anon, whose voice ran on
from Chaucer's Thames to Spenser's, deepening, strong:

Spenser Sweet Thames, run softly, till I end my song.

Narrator Then, rising higher,
the voice of Shakespeare:

Shakespeare Oh, for a muse of fire!

Narrator And Marlowe's, matching that sublime ascent:

Marlowe See, see where Christ's blood streams in the firmament.

Narrator I thought:

Ronald One day I too may spread
uncertain wings
to add, with what misgiving,
what fledgling quaverings,
notes of my own to that poetry which springs
from the dying lips of the living,
the living lips of the dead.

Narrator But these vain thoughts went whirling about
and turned to Flecker – lovely stuff to shout:

Ronald We are they who come faster than fate: we are they who ride
early or late:
We storm at your ivory gate: Pale Kings of the Sunset, beware!

Narrator I heard another voice, not in my head:

Ted (*Sturdy common sense*)
Have you gone off your blooming rocker?

Ronald Ted!

Ted You're barmy. Must be a touch of sunstroke, Ron.

Narrator I started to stammer:

Ronald I was thinking about Anon.
Chaucer, Spenser and Shakespeare.

Ted Oh, him. He's potty, like you.
I know. They made me read chunks of him at school.
(*Earnestly*) What good is poetry? Honest? Don't be a fool.
Study something useful. That's what you want to do.

Ronald (*Thinking it out as he goes*)
Oh, gosh, Ted. Poetry means everything in the world to me.
Look here. When I'm eighteen
I shall go on to university –
Oxford, I mean –
the only one, for me.

Just think of it. The city of dreaming spires...
of heights to scale.
I never told anyone this. It's my secret dream.
Oxford, to me, is like the distant gleam
of the Holy Grail,
the light that never was on sea or land.

Ted (*Honest bewilderment*) You're a rum lad.

Ronald (*Equally baffled on other side of fence*)
I want what Oxford can give me, don't you *see*?

Ted You'd meet chaps who knew what you were driving at, any road.

Narrator Like a blacksmith, he'd hit the iron while it glowed.

Ronald Yes, yes, Ted. As you and the keeper know
the ways of magpie, weasel, fox and stoat,
and recognise each wild bird by its note,
and tell the names of all the trees that grow,
and every flower in field, wood, or hedgerow.

Ted (*Not modesty: statement of fact*)
Keeper knows more than me.

Narrator So I told Ted, the simplest of souls,
something I thought he couldn't understand –
a secret I would not have told Hugh Moles,
who could, for naked shame.
Yet, in those flower-shot meadows by the mill-leet
I knew that Ted, bless him, had somehow sensed the heat
of the unshielded flame.
He said at the end of it, rising to his feet:

Ted Well, you're not that daft. It's time we had us tea.

Narrator And the weeks glided by.

Cuckoo Cuckoo. Cu-uckoo.

Narrator Like him, I haunted the river.

Cuckoo Cu-uckoo.

Narrator In July he must fly.
The surface of the flawed, greenish antique mirror
shivered. Beneath it went
the frantic, stark embodiment
of terror.
(*A distant otter hunt approaches*)
An otter, startled by the noise
of men and baying hounds and boys,
swimming, in silver seed-pearled fur

from those who were pursuing her,
keener than a whetted knife
a-flash in the sun, to have her life.
Through my deafness burst the brunt
of the hot, pursuing hunt.
(*The hunt passes them*)

Ted Ron, come on. Run, if you want to be in at the kill.

Narrator I pounded after him, heart a-thud,
to send, swift-coursing through my blood,
the deep, primeval hunting-thrill.
The village carrier, Bart,
with his plodding, philosophical Galloway
harnessed in the shafts of a smart flat cart,
carried parcels and gossip up and down Wensleydale.
Bart told, with relish, the tale
of how our Masham otter got away.

Bart (*Very broad speech*) She wor clever, that she wor.
Swam in under the roots of a sycamore
and t'unt went on ammost a mile, afore
they knew they'd been done an' dusted.

Narrator A lovely, inappropriate metaphor.
The huntsmen shut their ears to it, disgusted.
(*Pause*)
Time, like the otter, glided by
silently, through July.
Over flower-shot water-meadows
trees cast slightly longer shadows.
Cottage rose-plots breathed out musk
to bewitch the earlier dusk.
I lingered later in the shy light
of the owl-light, bat-light, twilight,
where Venus and the Pleiades
were tangled in the branchy trees.

One evening, I was drawn from these
up the hill to the market square,
by the magnet, Masham Fair.
(*Fade up Masham Fair*)
Harsh and hissing napthas threw
shadows softer than melting tar,

a shifting chiaroscuro,
restless as fever.
    (Bring up fairground steam organs)
The fairground organ's calliope-scream
raucous with tunes that everybody knew,
was counterpointed by the thud and jar
of the steam engine, driving the merry-go-round.
In the interplay of shadow, light and sounds,
the humdrum world of the village seemed estranged
from everyday reality, as though changed
by Puck, in a midsummer night's enchanted dream,
into the magic world of Bottom, the Weaver.
Unreason, light of heel,
in cap-and-bells,
for a brief, capering instant, chose to stand
by stolid reason near a roundabout, with a wheel
like a mangle's which was turned by hand.
A showman worked the mangle.
Round and round, with chubby legs a-dangle,
riding in shorts, or cotton frocks,
on carved and gilded hens and cocks
small children whooped.

Showman Roll up. Roll up. Penny a go.
Narrator The merry-go-round began to slow.
Hewson, a farmer to his boots,
his face as red as a boiled beetroot's,
cried:
Farmer Dosta want another go?
Narrator White-faced, the child shrieked:
Child No, no, no, no, no.
Narrator Hysteria made her blue eyes wide.
Hewson jingled his cash with pride.
Farmer Nay, then, my little Sal –
Tha's come to enjoy thissen – and enjoy thissen tha shall.
Gie her another tanner's worth.
Narrator The poor child's yells rent heaven and earth.
    (The child yells)
Ted You've stood treat, Ron. Now it's my turn.
Come on, look, I've money to burn.
Shillings a-plenty and to spare,

tanners, thruppenny bits, small change.
Let's have a go at the rifle range.

Narrator We did. And the darts. And the coconut shies.
We swung the swings to the starry skies.
Then a scream of fifes and a roll of drums:
(*Fifes scream and drums roll*)

Barker Johnny Bosco, here he comes.
Roll up. Roll up.

Narrator Up they rolled.
The carefree chaps, the would-be bold,
if somewhat sheepish in their bearing,
still, likely lads, not short of brass,
saved, penny by penny, since Candlemas,
to buy some bonny lass
a fairing.
(*Drums and fifes again*)
The lasses, sure enough, were there –
nut-brown dark or Saxon-fair,
some, timid as a crouching hare,
some, saucy hussies, bright-eyed, staring.
Half Wensleydale flocked, de'il-may-care
to spend its brass at Masham Fair.

Barker Roll up. Roll up for all you're worth
to see the strongest man on earth.
The great, the stupendous Johnny Bosco,
the champion, the world record-beater.
Juggler. Sword swallower. Fire-eater.
(*Drums*)
Bosco will now put on the show
all the crowned heads of Europe know
from the King of Spain to the Czar of Moscow.

Voice (*Jeering*) He's dead.

Barker (*Lightning retort*) He weren't in nineteen-ten.
Ladees and gentle-men
the genuine, the great, the tremendous,
the one and only Johnny Bosco.
(*Drums*)

Narrator Bosco's torso, stripped to the waist,
was impressively tattooed
with writhing dragons interlaced,

tigers and ladies in the nude.
Flat on his back on the cobblestones,
he laughed, as one who loves a jest,
when two men placed
across his breast
the wheel of an artillery limber.
Elm for the hub, oak for the spokes, ash for the felloes.
Seasoned timber
curlicued in scarlets and yellows,
it must have weighed an eighth of a ton.

Barker This wheel came from the limber of the gun
which fired the last shell on the Western Front.

Narrator An old sweat, leaning his back against the wall
spat tobacco juice and said:

Old Sweat Aye. And t' first shot in t' Zulu war an' all!
(*The crowd laughs*)

Barker Who's the heaviest man here?

Sam Me. Sam Hall. Twenty-six stun.

Barker Then stand on the wheel and Johnny will hoist thee up.
If he can't, tha'll get as much ale as tha can sup.

Voice Then God help t' White Bear.

Narrator Twenty-six stones of muscle, flesh and bones
balanced itself with massive confidence on the limber-wheel.
Bosco's tattooed dragons began
to ripple their scales of green and red.
Easily, Johnny hoisted wheel and man
two clear feet above his head.
Then tipped the wheel one way, the man the other.

Voice By gow – he mun be Samson's brother.

Narrator After that,
while the grinning barker went round with the hat
until its contents overspilt,
Bosco swallowed a flat sword to the hilt
as an ordinary mortal swallows a sprat.
He drew the sword out. With it came
from mouth and nostrils smoke and flame.
(*Final roll of drums*)

Sam Champion.

Voice That it wor, by heck.

Narrator Revellers, singing drunken songs,

reeled from pubs round the Market Square.
A feather, gripped by lazy tongs
suddenly tickled the back of my neck.
I whirled, and briefly glimpsed her there,
Round-eyed innocence, tumbled hair.
Light of foot, in and out
of the jostling throngs,
she fled.
I caught her near a roundabout.

Ronald Now then.
Rose Let me go.
Ronald When you've paid your forfeit.
Narrator She tossed her head.
Ronald I know you live here. What's your name?
Rose I'll pay my forfeit – maybe – if you find out.
Ronald You don't know what the forfeit is, so there.
Rose Yes I do. Take it – if you dare.
Narrator Beyond the naptha's garish glare,
in shadows lit by farthing dips,
she gave my wrist a sudden twist
and almost slipped my fingertips.
I swung her sideways by the waist,
my cheeks were brushed by her chestnut hair.
A greenhorn at this rustic game
my first shot missed –
then her warm, her moist, half-parted lips,
gave my first stolen kiss the taste
of the gilt on the gingerbread,
the touch of flame
when we clasped and kissed.
(*Fade fairground into distance*)
Down a lane where meadow-sweet scented the night breeze
we wandered, slowly, arms interlaced,
blissful, far from the madding fair,
and sipped of nectar, gathered where
the fields of heaven swarm with silver bees.
Cuckoo Cuckoo.
Narrator In August, go he must.
Cuckoo Cu-uck-oo.
Narrator And dying summer, with a dying fall,

strewed pot-pourri rose petals on the grass.
The yellow stonecrop shrank on the garden wall.
The mercury sank inside its thread of glass.
On my last evening, summer almost gone,
day drawing to its close,
I loitered with her, watching a sailing swan.
(*Fade up a river*)

Ronald A poet, more than two hundred years ago
knew your name before I did.
'Go, lovely rose.'

Rose (*Giggle*) It's quite good. It isn't one of the others, though
is it? You made it up yourself. Didn't you?

Ronald No.
That's Edmund Waller speaking. A quiet one.

Rose Not like you.
You're always talking poetry to me.

Ronald Because you're the very stuff of poetry.
'Go, lovely Rose' . . . yet you're staying in Masham, and it's I
who must go tomorrow. I'll think of you day and night.
Write to me, Rose. I'll write
I promise, every day.

Rose (*Straightforward*) No, Ronald. No. It's no use asking me why.
I like you – but everybody's laughing at me –
even my brother, Jeff,
for – for walking out with a boy who's deaf.
(*Pause*)
Honest, they've made my life a misery.
There's only Ted Ryder who'll stand up for you.
It's true.
None of them dare torment me when he's about.
They all know, if they do, he'll give them a clout.

Ronald (*Dazed*) But . . .

Rose It's no good. We can't go on.
I'm Wensleydale, Ron.
I'll never leave it and you won't come back.

Narrator Five minutes before, the river had seemed to catch
its breath at its own beauty. The mirrored swan,
alive as the real, so perfect was the match.
A shivering wind-flaw shattered the illusion.

Rose Don't look like that. I'm sorry – but, after all,

you don't belong here.
Narrator Across my blank confusion
there sprang, diagonally, a hair-line crack,
like the one I'd seen on the paint of a sick-bay wall.
I'd turned my face to that wall, not wanting to live.
Now, not meaning to, Rose had taught me that life can give
mind and emotion more hurt than physical pain.
I had not yet learned that all three are fugitive.
What Rose had said went stumbling through my head:
Rose (*Echoing from the past*) I like you, but everybody's laughing at me.
Narrator As, all my life at Crossley's, I had been
taunted and laughed at, for deafness – which was why
I'd longed so ardently to be fifteen.
Then I could stand up to them effectively.
I'd not foreseen
that deafness was a thing I'd have to fight
for the rest of my life, or give in to. Bitterly
I said to myself:
Ronald It isn't right. It isn't right,
it isn't fair. All girls will laugh at me.
They'll laugh at me at Oxford.
Narrator The voice of the river sang:
I smelled, as Rupert Brooke had smelled, the tang,
the dear, 'the thrilling sweet, and rotten
unforgettable unforgotten
river-smell' – were such things lies?
(*A brief but lingering chord from 'Irmelin' by Delius*)
Four rivers, men say, ran out of Paradise.
The fifth one flowed through Wensleydale, I think,
mingling these voices with its dragonflies,
as, at my summer's close, it made its way
between the bank of night, the bank of day,
while, cast from Eden, I tried to guess what lay
in store for me beyond the perilous brink
of that sweet summer
and, in sum,
of all the years to come.
I knew that time and the river would bear me on
as it had borne all poets since Anon,
past chestnut candles, lighting other fools

the way to dusty death,
the river of time with its deeps and shallows and pools.
I gulped one breath
then, turning, said:

Ronald Goodbye to Wensleydale.

Narrator A Shropshire Lad went with me and he said
in words which still re-echo in my head:

Housman The troubles of our proud and angry dust
Are from eternity, and shall not fail.
Bear them we can, and if we can we must.
Shoulder the sky, my lad, and drink your ale.

The Seasons of the Blind

The Seasons of the Blind was commissioned by the BBC to mark the centenary year of The Royal National Institute for the Blind and was first broadcast on Radio 4 on 22nd October 1968 with the following cast:

NARRATOR	*Michael Hordern*
PERSEPHONE	*Barbara Mitchell*
NIGHT	*Sheila Burrell*
MATT	*David March*
WINTER	*Francis de Wolff*
SUMMER	*Lisa Harrow*
AUTUMN	*Victor Lucas*

The many other parts were played by:
David Brierley, Wilfrid Carter, Jan Edwards, Nicholas Edmett, Leonard Fenton, Brian Haines, Kathleen Helme, Hilda Kriseman, Haydn Jones, Denis McCarthy, Lockwood West, Marjorie Westbury.

Produced by Charles Lefeaux

The play surveys the cycle of a year and shows how the blind must rely only upon memory and their remaining senses to appreciate the changing seasons.

> In my new radio play 'The Seasons of the Blind' I take one year of my own first crossing of the shadowy borderland between that country and the lands of sight... the setting of this adventurous exploration in the dark is my native county of Yorkshire, which I know so well and loved so much when I had the use of my eyes. Two cities, York and Sheffield, figure in the story, and the villages and people of the Dales.
>
> Could I, a countryman, leave out flowers, trees, rivers, birds, insects, beasts, fish, and the wheeling movement of the seasons? Spring, summer, autumn and winter are personified – as is night; is night my enemy? You will hear my answer in the play.

From an article by the author in Radio Times

Narrator Sleepless at midnight,
dreaming,
I thought the snowflowers burned
the purest of all candles . . .
Snowdrops To light Spring's dancing-floor.
Narrator Then swift and silver-seeming
Persephone returned . . .
Persephone With, in my hands, the locusts . . .
(*Fade up a distant swarm of locusts*)
Locusts Insatiable, to devour
green things in leaf and flower
as we have done before.
Narrator Your wings have darkened the skies of other Springs
my eyes now fading, have seen.
Have you not eaten your fill in the greenest years,
drunk of the sweetness of my heart's salt tears?
What more do you want of me?
(*The locusts louder*)
Locusts We are the locusts. We,
without pity, without hate,
inexorable, insatiate,
we, the locusts, devour all things green
feeding on sweetness in your bitterest hour.
Narrator Peresephone,
Goddess of Spring, Goddess of Hell,
ask of Truth in her secret well,
must this thing be?
Persephone Long since, with a shrug uncouth,
Pilate jested:
Pilate What is truth?
Persephone I, woman in her goddess-guise
doubly fear to meet Truth's eyes,
which mirror things as they are, not as they seem
in the world's half-light.
Close your own eyes and dream. The snowflowers dream
rooted in darkness. It is still midwinter.
A gale has driven the keel of the moon to splinter
on reefs of black cloud.

Sleep: it is deep night.
Narrator Night... dark rose...
Night Darkest rose...
Narrator And thorniest:
must those thorns pierce my sight?
Night (*Implacable certainty*) Darkness indeed must close.
Narrator But noon was blazing-bright...
Day showed me more than all your silver bees,
your swarms of fireflies,
remote, or tangled in the summer trees.
Day showed me birds in flight,
oh, lovelier than your singing Pleiades.
Day, ever-changing day
from dawn until you drained the dusk away.
Must I lose daylight? Lies, lies, lies, lies, lies.
Night (*Binding the spell*)
I, the flower of darkness,
petal on petal shall fold upon your eyes,
closing all other flowers, all other colours
within my own,
denying you delight
when summer lightfall is as autumn nightfall
and skies of spring the same as autumn skies.
Narrator Night, flower of darkness,
implacable enchantress,
in whose house I must dwell:
the spirit of man can face a grimmer starkness –
and I shall break your spell.
(*Music – 'The Walk to the Paradise Garden' by Delius*)
When I was young, when I was young,
when I was a boy in the North Country,
my mother, who had a vinegar tongue
and a heart of honey, said to me:
Mother Weave, weave from beauty's sudden gleams
a stuff more rare than cloth of gold,
the changing pattern of your dreams,
which may endure when you grow old...
Narrator Which shall endure and grow more bright
until the fading of all light.
Night Less than the flicker of a cosmic ray,

less than one fleck of foam in the frothed mill-race
of the Milky Way,
are the dreams of all men, sighted or unseeing,
to me in the gulfs of interstellar space
in which I live and move and have my being.

Narrator Dark rose,
you cannot fold me in the heart of darkness
for even in darkness I shall remember light.

Night (*Dismissively*) Dream your vain dreams.

Narrator In this grey light,
not that of day, not that of night,
as the shadows deepen more
and all sure footing's left behind,
against my will I must explore,
groping, the Country of the Blind.
(*Music – 'The Walk to the Paradise Garden' by Delius*)
The Walk to the Paradise Garden –
Delius.
He too was blind. His world of music sends
invisible allies, free, free, glorious,
across all frontiers to strengthen us
who stumble in darkness.
And then, to make amends
Sound Radio offers me
not poems I can't read, plays I cannot see,
but calms and tempests of a thousand voices
in which the inward eye, as the outer ear rejoices.
The voice of Edith Evans, saying so much
in two plain words...

Edith Evans A handbag?

Narrator The voice of Robert Donat,
full of the richness that is Shakespeare's own...

Robert Donat So hallowed and so gracious is the time.

Narrator Rich? I am rich in friends.
And, friends apart, I need no blind man's dog
to guide me night and day
through concrete jungles or a country lane,
perpetually trapped in Eliot's yellow fog
that rubs its nose against the window pane.
(*Three taps of stick*)

My white stick a swift divining-rod
which finds the hidden good in men.
I'd blithely travelled the shadowy borderland
a mile or two with, for companion, pride,
before he let me fall
near the white kissin-gate by the sandstone wall –
and pain flamed through my head like a searing brand.
Old Matt, with his slow, East Riding hedger's stride
by which he measured furlong, perch and chain,
loomed over me and said:

Matt Noo then, thoo needs a stick.
I'll mak thi yan.

Narrator Matt's hands were as seasoned as a piece of wood.
All things to do with the earth he understood,
and the ways of beasts in hill and dale and fen –
but not the ways of men.
Matt, like the earth, was never in a hurry,
but he knocked at my door one night:

Matt Here's stick Ah've made thi, lad. Ah've painted it white.

Narrator I like the feel of it. Thank you, Matt.
(*Tap and swish of stick in the air*)
It's light.
(*Three hard taps*)
And strong.
What wood is it?

Matt Wild cherry.

Narrator (*Alone*) Loveliest of trees, the cherry now ...
I'll see no bloom along the bough
all about the woodland ride
next, or any Eastertide ...
(*More resolutely*)
But now, since needs must, I will go
and tap my way through real snow.
(*Footsteps crunching and stick slurring snow*)
The last snow of the old year ...
(*Sloppy splash*)
half thawing into slush.
(*Tap on wall*)
A hundred and ten paces. Turn left here.
The air smells raw. No traffic in the street.

(*Distant singing in a tap-room*)
Ah, tap-room voices.
Soon I'll feel the heat
through the snowflakes swirling and stinging
and . . . yes . . . I can hear what they're singing.

Tap room (*In rollicking voice*)
Come, come, come and make eyes at me
Down at the old Bull and Bush.

Tap voice (*Calling, jovial*) You're late to-neet.

Narrator Who's that?

Tap voice (*Hurt*) You know me, Ned Barker.

Narrator I'll look in later.
(*Vaguely apologetic*) I'm going up the hill.

Tap voice You're never going to church? On New Year's Eve?
Nay, bugger it.
(*Roar of laughter*)
(*Tap and crunch-slush of steps again*)

Narrator (*Alone*) They must think I've taken leave of my senses.
I suppose the night's still darker,
no stars to see, if I could.
(*Steps stop*)
How still, how still
the village is.
(*Pause. Harder taps*)
The church wall . . . and the tower
about there . . . I will wait,
I won't go in, but stand in the lychgate
until the hour.
Yes, yes, I'll use the tower for a marker
from which to find my way
in the Country of the Blind for a year and a day.
A hundred thousand of my fellow blind
have learned the laws its subjects must obey –
and on this pilgrimage I too may find
that, like the Arctic, it holds exhilaration
for the bold spirit
under the glow of the Northern Lights of the mind.
(*The hoot of an owl*)
Midnight is near,
brooding over the tower.

(*A pause of absolute silence*)
For full five centuries
the hands of the masons
that builded the tower . . .

Masons (*Remote, tranquil*) . . . have rested from labour,
folded, still.

Narrator Still, in the belfry,
bronze shoulder to shoulder,
the bells in their cradles
rest, motionless, silent
in the night's chill.
Chill, the great bell ropes
plunge downwards through darkness
sheer fifteen fathoms
to the hands of the ringers . . .

Ringers . . . waiting, until
we grasp the sallies
and

Chief Ringer Pull.

(*Church bells peal for the New Year*)

Narrator And clamour
and jubilation
from baying bell-mouths
from parish to parish
their tongues' wild music
make men's hearts thrill.
My heart turns over like the bells
so loud they ring, so clear.

Village voices Happy New Year . . .
New Year . . .
New Year.

(*The bells fade. Pause*)

Narrator Plough Monday, Matt.

Matt Aye. When I was a lad
we used to drag t'owd plough up village street.
There wor St George
and there wor t' Dragon an' t'Doctor
wi' a gurt bottle o' medicine, that powerful-strong
it 'ud lift dead fro' their graves.
'Here be I' wor my piece.

'Here be I, little Dairy Doubt,
wi' my shirt tails hanging out.'
If squire didn't gie us a barrel of ale
us ploughed his lawn up for him!
(*Laughs deep and long*)

Narrator No St George now, and no free barrels of beer
but plenty of dragons, Matt.
Well – I'm off up the lane.
Most of the snow's gone, hasn't it?

Matt Most on it.
It'll hang aboot – there wor a black frost last neet.
(*Tap of stick, hard*)

Narrator Now the startled morning sun
sees what ill work by night was done.
Ice stills all blood's quick-coursing flow
daunting the fox and the carrion crow,
the Denchman, he, the Danish man...
(*The croak of a carrion crow*)
Wish I could see as far as you can,
old bloody-beak.
(*Shivers*) Ah, the East wind's bitter.
Frost, a Black Prince with eyes a-glitter,
in the gauntlet-grip of his iron hand
grasps the throat of the conquered land.
(*Stick taps*)
A lull in the wind? Ah, the sun feels good.
I'm in the lee of Ghost Owl Wood.
(*The song of a robin sharp and clear*)
Sing, robin, fill your throat
with frosty air and pipe your note,
for rests the harrow and rusts the plough,
and all birds else are silent now.
(*The robin again*)
But what are you doing here? The worm casts harden
until they're fossils.
Fly to my neighbour's garden,
his children will feed you crumbs.
(*Brief robin song*)
How the weeks drag. But February comes.
(*The distant yells and shrieks of children*)

With yells and shrieks the children scoop
fire-shovelfuls of snow
and fling them on the mounding heap,
clipped shearings of old winter's sheep.
They shout and jump, they run and leap
to see the Snowman grow.
And he shall have my old burnt pipe
black-carbonised...

Neighbour's wife And, lawks!
a dustbin hat, all green-mould grey.

Neighbour The gloves the scarecrow threw away,
and for his comfort...

Neighbour's wife Well-a-day!
the muffler of Guy Fawkes.

Narrator And children, blasé, weep hot tears, heartfelt,
when unabominable snowmen melt.
And underneath earth's tattered winding-sheet
life, germinating, stirs in the winter wheat.
And my heart lifts at a high, far sound...
(*The wing beat and the cry of wild swans pass*)
Wild swans!
Their out-thrust necks like swords of Roman bronze,
I see them, in my mind's eye, making wing
over pastures, naked woods and ploughland-swell
whose names in memory sing.
Over the flooding Wharfe and Burnsall Fell –
but not yet North, North, North, at the call of Spring.
(*Fade up a cold wind*)
Year after year, with engines dread,
Winter lays siege to Snowgatehead.
A farm – a cottage – and naught else
save naked sky and naked fells,
most beautiful and as austere
as abstract truth in a man's head,
and yet as real as concrete,
as boulder rock to booted feet.
The sleet comes over the fell crests
driven as from arbalests.
Frost engineers a grim device:

Frost A catapult with thews of ice

I mount in every watercourse.
Narrator The blizzard strikes:
Blizzard With javelin force.
Narrator Against stone walls King Winter slams:
Winter The four winds, blunt battering rams,
and as they drive home blow on blow
my redan outworks of the snow,
foot by swallowing drift-foot creep
closer to the folded sheep.
Narrator But wall and rafter, stone and wood
for three centuries have stood
such assaults; and this will fail
though mounted upon such a scale,
for the beleaguered's hardihood,
native to their Northern blood,
fortifies their certain hope.
They see, from their high Pennine slope,
beyond the fell, below the scree,
what we, sheltered, do not see –
(*The wind fades*)
the vanguard of advancing Spring
which another month may bring
to lift the siege of Snowgatehead.
They shall find hill-flowers spread
small but delicate, sparse but sweet,
before the destined Conqueror's feet.
(*Music – A harp arpeggio*)
Narrator Spring comes to the South as music to the harp,
but to the North, as a trumpet heard in the hills.
(*A trumpet, distant and faint*)
The hill beck spills
and the first blackbird sings.
(*Sing up blackbird*)
(*Calling*) What are you shouting at, Blackbird?
Blackbird Parson Rook with the pale sun for candle.
Rook (*Distant*) And for book
and bell as well.
The ice-clink brook
uttering a commination
on scandal in the congregation.

(*Rookery in full caw, then fading*)

Narrator (*Mocking*) 'Aw 'eck, 'aw 'eck, 'aw 'eck.
Much respectable sinners reck
in chapel or church (or the elms by the beck)
of sermon, text or peroration.
(*A joyous burst of blackbird*)
Blackbird, you pagan!
(*Sharp tinkle of cat-ice*)
Cat-ice, brittle as glass.
I'll follow the cart-track over the first-bite grass.
I'll kneel and stroke
the crispy turf. (*Pause*)
A daisy. And another.
And three. Oh, Holy Mother
of God, five daisies.
If you can cover five daisies with the sole of your foot,
it's Spring.
(*Pause. He sniffs*)
I smell wood-smoke – it tells of gipsies.
(*Quiet, menacing snarl of a lurcher dog*)

Bosco (*Romany, not the wheedling sort except when he wants to sell something*)
Bitte (*pronounced: bitty*) tan, bori yog.

Narrator Bosco!
(*Snarl, more subdued*)
And that's your lurcher dog.

Bosco A bitch. Heel, Beshli. Kushti bok.

Narrator I know that one: 'Good luck.'
What's bitte tan, bori yog?

Bosco (*Chuckle*) Little camp, big fire.
My vardo's there – my waggon . . .
touched up for Shipley Fair.
First of the Yorkshire fairs, as Nidderdale Rant
at the back end's the last.

Narrator Ah – the Romany and hoar-frost never stay
in the same place after nine days have passed.

Bosco That's what you think.
I've wintered near the copperworks, Stourton way
Three railway embankments for shelter –
and naught to pay.

Narrator What's that you're shaving with your plane?
Bosco I'm making an illusion. A disembodied head.
We must educate the public. (*Laughs*)
Narrator Then you'll take the road?
Bosco Aye: jall the drom.
Narrator God, how I envy you.
Harried like pariah dogs
by little tin gods with the manners of hogs –
but you can follow what remains
of uphill, downhill, roundabout lanes –
Fridaythorpe, Yockenthwaite, Appletreewick –
where once I went with pipe and stick.
Appletreewick, where white clouds sail
over the deep and narrow dale
in a sky of starling's eggshell blue
– as here and now I know they do.
(*Linnets sing*)
And now the linnets sing.
Bosco, the lyric spring is mine,
with air sharp-sweet as dandelion wine.
(*Abruptly*) I'm off to the river.
Bosco Kushti bok.
(*Music – 'On hearing the first cuckoo in Spring' by Delius*)
(*Then a running brook and a blackbird*)
Narrator All day the blackbird in the linden tree
lifts up his orange bill and shrieks with glee:
Blackbird Look, look, the grass is green, green, green.
Not in seven seasons have I seen
the leaves so lyrical – and look, look, look
there goes Jack Hodgson's boy ...
Boy (*Whistling back at blackbird*) Down to the brook.
Blackbird Look, look –
Narrator The blackbird shouts:
Blackbird The sky's blue, blue,
the sun has burned a golden peephole through
the floor of heaven for all the saints to see
the wonder the world is.
Narrator So, all day, to me
the blackbird shrieks. And I, who have not seen
these things for years, know that the grass is green

exactly as he says, and full of joy
whistle with blackbird and Jack Hodgson's boy.
And on a happier day
buds on the trees of April are leaves on the trees of May.
(*Fade brook into music – 'On hearing the first cuckoo in Spring' by Delius*)
Trees live in light:
light flows in subtle waves
along each branch,
engulfs each leaf.
Oh, perfect day of May, with light imbued,
the hedges bursting and the grass thick-dewed
spangled with cuckoo-spit.
(*A cuckoo interrupts the music*)
The froghopper ejected it,
not you!
Most inconspicuous of insects, grey
architect of Xanadu,
builder in light-imprisoning foam
more delicate than honey-dew,
dweller in miraculous glass,
how do your marvellous hours pass?

Froghopper The dark bird, Death,
the black bird, Death
may suddenly
destroy my universe and me.
Look through my myriad lenses. What do you see?

Narrator Death. Omnipresent death.
I see death, the shrike, the butcher bird, striking . . .

Death . . . a linnet's breast on the thorns
of a quickset hedge.

Narrator I see death, the weasel . . .

Death . . . sucking blood from the throat
of a young rabbit and discarding it
like a glove-puppet.

Narrator I see death, the diving otter, silvered
over sleek fur with underwater bubbles. . .

Death . . . which burst, as the grayling's gills
burst in my teeth.

Narrator I see death, the mole . . .

Death ... grasping a headless worm in my
gravedigger's hands
to drag to a torture pit already full
of other headless worms,
my living meat.

Narrator These things I see through your
thousand windows, froghopper –
and brown men, red men, black men, yellow men
in lands of morning and in lands of midnight
– three thousand million refracted images
of my own face, froghopper, my own race.
(*Fade up random early summer bird song*)
Yet I am wrong. We are more cruel than they.
We talk of brutes. What do the animals say?

Animals We share your world, but neither criticise
your attitude to us, nor analyse
your motives for behaving as you do.

Blackbird Bird...

Weasel Weasel ...

Otter Otter ...

Animals We are aware of you
to the exact extent, or more, or less,
that you intrude upon our consciousness;
our senses are both keener and more blunted
than yours. We are the hunters and the hunted
and therefore lead immediate lives.

Weasel Your narrow world...

Blackbird ... which you imagine vast...

Animals ... is bounded by the future and the past, while we...

Ladybirds ... and ladybirds...

Trees ... and trees...

Flowers ... and flowers...

All live in the infinite present, which is ours,
with appetites on edge, or satisfied,
but integrated, whole, unclassified...

Otter Alive...

Weasel Alone...

All Drawing, as you draw, breath.

Narrator Yet, oh distinction, unaware of death!
Not knowing, the wolf-spider in the grass,

the ravenous pike with his cold eyes of glass,
the snail on the wall, the seed in the pregnant earth,
that there is any mystery in birth.
(*Sighs*) Innocent ourselves, we are the fruit of the Tree
of the knowledge of good and of evil.

Blackbird (*Child-like curiosity*)
Does it taste bitter, son of Adam, or sweet?

Narrator I know the name of it only: ecstasy –
and no man knows
when it will come to him, when it will go.

Soul But I, the soul, the dove,
know when it comes
and what it is:
light, light, light, pure light.

Persephone By which we half-immortals likewise live.

Narrator Persephone, you came to wintry earth . . .

Persephone . . . and you could cover
five daisies with one shoe.

Narrator Oh, wonderful, I said . . .

Persephone . . . and a thousand miracles happened,
and each enchanted you.
The morning skies were grey, the evenings red.
There came cowslips and buttercups
everywhere that the grass grew.
The grass, and the hundred different kinds of grass,
flowered and seeded, lived in air and light,
drank dew, and gripped the earth with roots:
froghoppers frothed their domes of Xanadu glass,
alarms of fire disturbed the ladybirds,
butterflies played their masques,
the crickets beat their drums,
hares brushed the thick dew with their thicker fur.

Narrator Ah, do not lift your spell, Persephone:
say 'Not yet summer, not yet the reaper comes.'

Persephone (*Capriciously*) I'll stay . . .
as long as chestnut candles blaze at noon –
I'll stay as long
as the chaffinch takes
relearning his mating song . . .
(*A chaffinch sings*)

I'll stay, perhaps I'll stay
until the bees desert the orchard trees...
(*Bees hum*)
I'll stay, I'll stay –
and go when flower-o'-May
melts from the hawthorn beneath the young June moon.

Narrator Not yet: oh, linger on...
It was but yesterday
that children parted the hair of the grass to find
the first faint violet,
and shouted when an April rainbow shone
above the rainy woods
in a shivery wind which shook the sticky buds,
it was but yesterday: stay, stay.

Blackbird She's gone.

Narrator Gone. Gone...
(*Music – Overture to 'A Midsummer Night's Dream' by Mendelssohn*)
On Housman's idle hill of summer
now I hear the steady drummer
drumming in a wood of dreams.
(*Music faded*)
Summer. Demeter, the Corn Goddess,
the mother of Persephone,
wide-eyed, walking listlessly.
Where day-dreaming summer goes...

Summer ... there enchanter's nightshade grows. Listen...
(*Fade up a summer river*)
The drowsy river flows
with vague, meandering music lulling
the greensleeve noon, that hardly knows
which way the perfume of the rose
floats on the air, which way the notes...

River (*Speaking, as the fish does in 'Sparkie' bubbling through water*)
Nor, at the long cadenza's close,
if flower or tune... were worth... the culling.

Summer Smooth as a billow of the Glassy Sea
but full of liquid colour –
grape-bloom blue,
waterweed-green and green of the ash-key –
beside the willow-shiver

flows my enchanted river,
past Collingham Bridge to Wetherby it slides,
in tranced, swan-glides.
Beside the landing stage the mirroring river
rocks all its images.
Into this quiet water-spell's hushed dreaming,
young Marc projects himself and his canoe.
For him the tranquil river-world is teeming . . .

Marc With things to hear
and touch
and see and do –
especially *do*.

Summer His brown, eight-year-old body,
as supple as a salmon's
knows the feel
of the canoe-shell riding the rimpling water.
To either side he flashes
the uplifted blade, agleam with running pearls.
He laughs aloud
at the shock of the showery splashes.
There are cattle knee-deep in the shallows
to be greeted.

Marc Hello, cows. Moo, there, moooooo.

Summer And lo a streak of long blue lightning darts . . .

Marc Kingfisher, kingfisher!

Summer His lovely flight completed
the lightning sleeps on the bewildered air
one dazzled moment, still remaining there.

Narrator (*Sudden outburst*) I've drugged myself with beauty I cannot see.
I cannot see. I cannot see. I'm blind.
Light, colour, movement, everything I love,
the face of love itself, I cannot see.
I am condemned to walk in darkness for life.
(*Long pause*)
(*More calmly*) An angel stooped but yesterday:
ere I had time to shield my sight
the shadow of his wing fell grey
between all colour and the light.
In the penumbra of his wing
blind Milton's gum my gaze must clog.

Vague shapes to which dim meanings cling
move in a never-ending fog.
I said at first: 'My inward eye
shall blaze with such an angry flame,
that, burning through the day's black sky,
it shall search out that angel's name.
I will appeal against the shade
of darkness. Lord, this is not just.'
The angel's voice one answer made:

Angel Be silent, noisy grain of dust!
Can you tell what seems to be
from what is truth, by mortal sight?
The shadow of my wing may lift –
and dazzle you with too much light.

Narrator (*Triumph*) These eyes of mine,
which missed so much,
have been
blessed by the sight
of the soul itself of light.
For I have seen
the wind's fingers running arpeggios
of ripples over the river,
and at their touch
so clear the water was,
vibrating bands,
Greek fires of rhythms through the water ran.
Brandywine brown, with shadows of soft tar
beneath the pebbles,
the river ran that day.
It ran beneath a tunnel of sky and trees,
trees greener than the heart itself could say
were it to cry:

Heart I love you, green, above all other colours.

Narrator So would my heart have said –
but for the Greek-fire gold in the brandy water,
and then,
oh then, the water-shadows played
over a sycamore made that blessing fuller.
Diastole,
systole,

flames of pure light beat over the tree,
contracting, dilating, flickering free,
running up bole and branch and twig
and down again and over each fig
shape of a leaf, until the whole tree
burned with frore flames, burned with living light, and lived.
I praised God I had received
so blest a sight
in recompense
for the failure of my sense
so often, in not seeing clear
enough His Works. I would hold dear
indeed the price, if I were told
that any mortal, young or old,
could behold
with living eyes that living light,
that burning-bush-of-glory tree –
and yet not see, and yet not *see*.
(*Long pause*)
I think men saw more clearly in the days
before they wore spectacles
to gape at a spectacle.
As still they see more clearly in a village
than in a concrete jungle.
Most clearly, I believe, in river villages –
say in Cawood. Farther down-river
the Cardinal's palace –
what time has left of it –
dreams by the Ouse.
Wolsey, the butcher's lad,
he was bereft of it,
he who could choose
abbey and bishopric at his own pleasure.
Voices of villagers drinking their ale
take up the tale
of the spell that he cast.
Voices that mingle with voices that hang
in the roof of the raftered past.
Voice Wolsey could measure
the worth of a span

of fat oxen –

Voice The yield
of corn uncut in the field –

Voice The price of a farm –

Voice Or a man –

Voice Aye – to a groat
– prince, or varlet.

Voice Squat, powerful, enigmatic,
he sat there in scarlet, intriguing, whispering –

Voice Keeping in Cawood more state than the king.

Narrator Grey village the cardinal knew . . .
Dream. Barges drift,
loaded with grain.
Lift, Cawood, lift
broad voices, now as then,
talking of loss or of gain.
Power passes. Corn – and what Yorkshire calls brass –
the river, the land: these remain,
and women, and talk of women: these do not pass.
The cardinal's farms remain –

Voice Aye, known to this day for the pick of the fat of the plain
all round the palace of Cawood, broad acres and orchards
plumpty.

Narrator But little remains of the palace of Humpty-Dumpty:
a granary; part of the gatehouse archway
with the room where he sat
in his cardinal's robes and his archbishop's workaday hat
and his great ring and all,
watching out, uncertain, in doubt,
waiting for the king's horses and all the king's men,
and his great fall.

Small girl (*Singing unaccompanied*)
And all the king's horses and all the king's men
couldn't put Humpty-Dumpty together again.

Narrator Does she know whose epitaph she sings? Not she!
I hear her run to the side of the bridge to see
a cabin cruiser, like a gay lady, glide
up-river for York on the striding morning tide.
She'll anchor, as like as not, by Guildhall's water-stair,
fast by the Roman arch of Stonegate, where

in the bright Dark Ages, men we might have known,
lived, loved and worked – and thought in terms of stone.

Quarryman I cut stone for a living –
Narrator the quarryman said.
Roadmaker I break stones...
Narrator said the road-maker...
Roadmaker ... partly to earn my bread –
partly to make roads for all men.
Narrator The mason bent his head –
Mason I build in stone to the glory of God.
Narrator And all are dead.
Up the street called Stonegate came
by road, from narrow riverbarge,
stone to build the Minster's frame,
and pillars like grey, stone-stilled flame
for nave and transept –
to enlarge
the spirit of man
by the strong hands of the artisan.
Yet stands the wall; the tower stands;
flying buttress, mullion, roof.
Time, greyer than stone, makes hard demands.
Time I test man's work to probe its proof.
Narrator And Time has found a weakness here,
undermining tower and pier.
Still through the great rose window streams
daylight made rich by dead men's dreams.
Reverence still imparts a bloom
to the founder's simple tomb.
The lintel of the Chapter House
still informs the lettered mouse:
Scholar (*Pedantic, slow*) 'Ut rosa, phlos phlorum
ista domus domorum.'
Narrator 'As the rose is flower of flowers
so is this the house of houses.'
I walk where peace, long centuried, drowses
between the organ swells of hours.
Men pour out copper, silver, gold
that wall may stand and tower hold;
the rose of love, and that alone

can heal the weakness in the stone –
for love it is which prompts such gifts.
In shadow, I sense how daylight shifts
through the Five Sisters' grisaille glass.
Here minutes like hours, like seasons, pass,
ruby-glowing, or grey-pearled,
heedless in their timelessness
of the strident outside world.
I climb the long stair
to the Minster roof
where the air chills –
there's autumn in this air.
If I could see again, how I would stare
as roundly as, down there,
the Eye of Yorkshire, Clifford's Tower, would stare
round the three Ridings, if it, too, could see.
Imagination, the mind's eye, shows to me
to the South-West,
Sheffield, truculent, downright, arms akimbo
her mouth a-tilt, the honest tart
who gives each man what he pays for.
Sheffield sprawls among those hills,
her skirts bedraggled in limbo,
her head in frowsy shawls by day,
by night her throat bedecked
with necklaces of rubies, fire-flecked,
and duller garnets
and beads of street-lamp gold –
jewels bought for her by the sweat and thirst
of furnacemen who laughed and spat and cursed
as the ladled steel poured from the crucible
in a blinding arc, a white-hot molten burst.
There was my cradle, in the tough steel city,
up to snuff, football-crazy,
knowing not the word 'lazy'
but aware of the meaning of pity.
There, where my life began,
the incandescent cataracts leapt and ran,
through delta channels of black foundry sand,
and cooled and crept like glaciers,

and began
to change their colours down the spectrum band.
I left her long ago –
but with her hall-mark
stamped on my shoulder,
worn smoother, alas, I know
as I grow older.
Eheu, is it autumn already?

Autumn Nay, whoa, lad, steady,
what's wrong with me to make a stout heart quail?
Come, take a sup of my October ale,
brewed Masham way, or happen in Wensleydale.
You'll find my best October amber-mellow.
Come, Autumn is an easy-going fellow:
Let's walk through Hackness woods and Glaisdale forest
and on towards the Esk where it nears the sea.

Narrator I'll walk with you, Autumn, through Glaisdale, willingly.

Autumn The green of all leaves is duller,
but flecked and streaked with colour.
(*The distant barking cough of deer*)
There are red deer in Glaisdale and their coats
grow thicker.
(*The call of cock pheasants*)
The cock pheasants swell their throats
and strut like gamecocks. Listen.
(*Leaves stir in the forest*)

Narrator A murmuration, a susurration:
like the sea-sound, which deceives
when a sea-shell is pressed to the ear.
The wood uneasily heaves . . .

Autumn Sensing the turn of the year.
Listen – and you will hear . . .

Narrator The four winds in the trees.
Soon, the trees say:–

Trees (*Sighing*) Our leaves will fall like spray.

Autumn Bronze,
bronze as a Saxon shield,
amber as beads of old,
rusty as ancient greaves,
yellow as Viking gold,

in forest and wood and field
will swirl and eddy the leaves.

Narrator Their smell
pervasive, earthy, cold –
and Time with weight of him presses
the once-gay, the once-green dresses,
into leaf-mould.

Autumn These have not yet come to that end.
On, on to Esk, my friend.
Esk slides, olive green,
between
her sycamored, her aldered banks.
Few oaks grow near
the mouth of Esk –
woodmen dead this many a year,
felled them.

Woodmen For the ribs and flanks,
the counters and blunt bows grotesque
of whalers manned by Russup men.

Whalers Whitby men and Russup men
harder than the ice we rammed.

Autumn Sheltered under St Hilda's hills
Whitby men are hardy still –
hardy as the seabirds.
(*Fade up sea on a rocky coast with cormorants*)
On that over-jetting ledge,
at the edge
of the sea's recoil and shock,
Cormorant, are you bird or rock?
Or were you cast in classic bronze,
still and tense, like an Amazon's
dusky body, bowstring-taut?
Arrow-swift
as your own thought
through spindrift
and waves which strive
to mash the pounded cliff, you dive.
In the North Sea, sleet, spume and snow
sky, storm and coming winter get to grips.
You match in courage men who go

down to the sea in ships.

Narrator The sea, that now prepares to launch the assault
of Winter on the land.

Autumn And I, like the ragged, claret-clad troops of the heather
must beat the retreat.
(*Fade up wildfowl in autumn migration*)
Listen –

Narrator Mallard . . . and widgeon . . . and shearwater
coming down from the North . . .
(*Fade up strongly, wild geese in flight*)
and geese, a skein of wild geese.
They seek their winter quarters . . .
and I seek . . .

Autumn What do men seek?

Narrator Men? What do men not seek?
But I believe that somewhere in all men
there is . . . the unknown poet, who may speak
or remain silent, perhaps unrecognised
save at rare moments, inarticulate.

Autumn Is poetry a thing in the minds of men –
to me, the most mysterious of the animals?
Why are they not content, as the others are,
to be born, to mate and to die?
(*Wild geese again*)

Narrator Ask of the wild geese, and they with their souls in their winging:
would they stoop in their flight from the North, for farmyard
fare?
Is not the falling star to burn the answer?
These go where they must go, seek what they must seek –
And so must I, a poet, seek for beauty,
or I die within my spirit.

Autumn Son of Adam,
seasons, like men, must die at Time's appointment.
My spirit, which is as old as Nineveh,
as young as Greece, warns me my hour is near.
(*Jovially*) Be with me in the spirit when I pass –
perhaps at Nidderdale Rant,
or Appleby Fair.

Narrator Ah, many's the friend of mine I'd meet with there.

Singer To Appleby in Westmorland

I take a chestnut mare.
(The quiet clip-clop of a horse)
The roads dip in, the roads climb out,
the shallow river, full of trout,
sings, purls and ripples round about
its green-cupped fields, and there –
Chorus We hold the Autumn Fair.
Singer To Appleby, in Westmorland,
go mugs and sharps and flats
and mares that plod and colts that prance
and girls as gallant as a lance
and dealers hard of countenance
as their black bowler hats.
(Fade up horse fair, whinneys, tramplings)
First fair voice *(Sneering, utter disparagement)*
Roach-backed, ewe-necked, Roman-nosed,
splay-footed, hip-shot, wi' bellows to mend
an' she's gotten a wall-eye, greasy-leg, the botts
and the blind staggers.
Second fair voice *(A friend of the sneerer who wants to buy the horse)*
Aye; an' bishoped an' all; a Yorkshire five,
past mark o' mouth if ivver I claped e'en on one.
Third fair voice *(Tolerant refutation of time-worn charges)*
She's mark o' mouth, her wind is sound.
Stand back, there: I'll move her round.
(A thunderous pound of hooves)
First fair voice *(As one maddened by his own recklessness)*
I'll gie thi – forty.
Third fair voice *(Implacable)* Ninety-five.
And there's my hand.
First fair voice Nay, man alive!
Third fair voice *(Reminiscently)* I gave the farmer back a pound
for luck, when our hands clasped and bound
the bargain – but, I swear,
I almost wished I hadn't found
a buyer at the fair.
(The horse fair fades)
Narrator Where are you, Autumn? Where?
(A tawny owl cries)
Tawny Owl Tu whit . . . tu where, tu where?

Narrator The tawny owl. How well I know that screech.
Old Autumn went to sleep at the foot of a beech,
and beeches love cold ground.
There, in the night, ground frost, the white vampire, found
and finished him.

Ground Frost I come by night, more silently than Night,
choosing the moon-chilled currents of the air
down which to steal.
Where the spider spun her wheel
in the ditch, beside the dead nettle,
and over hedge and field, I, Ground Frost, settle.
The owl knows me for an ally, for I numb
her prey's quicksilver senses
so delicately they know not I am come.
The still moon sees my work as it commences.
The tawny owl, the horny-eyed . . .

Tawny Owl . . . sees it . . . and is satisfied.
'Tu whit, tu who –

Narrator a merry note
While greasy Joan doth keel the pot.'

Winter Those lines are Shakespeare's –
I, Winter, understood
his Winter's Tale,
as Shakespeare knew, in his coursing English blood,
the tempest and the gale.
(*Fade up a storm at sea*)
Full well he knew my sea-jarls, roisterous –

Sea Jarls Drunk on salt spindrift, roaring,
with tempers as boisterous
as wind and waves.

Winter They come, as they came of old, at my command
singing their sagas, while the wind in the rigging rails
at my black ravens on their longship's sails.

Sea Jarls Land to the Sou-West, land!

Winter Beach each ship and follow me
wading ashore through the seething sea,
my terrible ice-sword, Landwaster,
a-whirl in my berserker hand.
(*Fade sea but keep wind*)

Narrator Old pagan Winter raves;

earth's children cower.
In the old sandstone wall beside my house
sleet, snow, wind and frost have carved out intricate caves
and crevices moss-lined by the shivering mouse.
They are proof against rough waves
of winter-winds, gale-tossed.
There are crevices too small for the weasel's shaky head,
too deep for the paw of a cat
who hears within, quick hearts going pit-a-pat.
There are small birds huddled there, pressed
warm breast to feathered breast.
(*Faint cheeping of small birds in a confined space*)
I hear their faint cheep-cheeping as I pass
my white stick tapping, skidding on the children's ice-slide glass
as I make my difficult way
towards The Fox.
(*Fade up inn chatter*)

Matt Come on, lad: I've a pint lined up for thee.

Narrator Who's that?

Matt Nay, thoo knows me, lad: it's Matt.
Three days to Kersmass.

Narrator So . . . there's room at the inn?
He claps my shoulder – and I sense his grin.

Matt Fooils don't believe i' Kersmass –
but I do,
the Kings and the Shepherds. I wor a shepherd yance.
It's easy to believe, on Staxton Hill
beneath t' breet stars in Kings, and Angels too.

Village voice That's daft – there's no angels!
(*A burst of guffaws fading*)

Narrator (*Alone*) Are there no angels? Then explain
how long on earth man could remain
without the warning angel, pain?
That Angel of the Agony.
(*Distant church bells*)
And now it's Christmas Eve
and village voices echo in the street –

Voice A Merry Christmas . . .

Voice . . . Christmas.

Voice Merry Christmas.

Narrator Soft snow on my face? or sleet?
The angels, the shepherds, the kings:
no room for them now at the inn?
But who am I to judge,
who am the son of a woman,
what other men believe
on Christmas Eve?
Whether her heart be tranquil,
whether her heart be wild
in the Night of forebeing
before the birth of her child,
woman sees without foreseeing
how far and in what ways
with, or without what friend
her child will walk Life's quickset maze
to what veiled end?
Thus, in pain and elation,
woman, wise or ignorant,
draws near to the radiant,
the central flame of creation,
at the birth of her child.
As in church on Christmas Day
Christians sing of light's pure ray
relit in Adam's lamp of clay.
(*A verse of the carol 'O Come all ye faithful' is sung*)
As well as gold and frankincense and myrrh
what counsel did the Magi offer her
who bore the Christ Child?

Caspar I, Caspar, King of the Roof of the World and wise
with the wisdom of great age in my sunken eyes,
I say,
Lullay, lullay,
in his mother's arms
let him wake, sleep, smile,
safe from all harms
for a brief while.

Balthasar I, Balthasar, King of the Middle Earth
who dices with jewels, regardless of their worth,
I say
Lullay, lullay,

let him sleep secure,
those arms hold fast
the cynosure
of all our past.
His fingers, curled,
seek instinct's clue.
Child, you grope for the world
men made for you.

Melchior I, Melchior, King of Earth's desert places
in whose blue veins youth's quick blood hotly races,
I say
Lullay, lullay,
a surer guide
than instinct lies
sealed, Child, in your wide
unfocused eyes.

Three Kings Born to err,
like you, we grope
for once we were
what you are – hope.
Sleep, Child, and wake –
we gave you birth –
and for love's sake
hope walks the earth.

Narrator Hope walks the earth, despite
despair and evil.
(*Music – a Chopin nocturne, suggesting starlight*)
I have lost my fear of you, light.
I have journeyed through the Country of the Blind
while the wheel of the Seasons turned.
I have discerned
that its black shadows merely emphasise
for my blind fellow-travellers' inward eyes
the contours of the Country of the Mind.

Night (*Part resentful, part curious*)
Who taught you my myriad eyes are not as bright
as the eyes of man's insight?

Narrator 'Rose, dark rose,
darkest rose and thorniest' – Night,
you taught me.

Night, you made me wonder in
darkness and silence, why the pointers pin
the tip of the Great Bear's tail with a diamond brooch to the Pole.
Dark rose, you stir the wonder in man's soul.
(*The nocturne ends. Pause. Then the cry of a tawny owl*)
New Year's Eve again.
Chill, the great bell-ropes
plunge downwards through darkness
sheer fifteen fathoms
to the hands of the ringers
waiting, until –

Ringers We grasp the sallies and . . .

Chief Ringer Pull.
(*Church bells peal*)

Narrator . . . and clamour
and jubilation
from baying bell mouths
from parish to parish
their tongues' wild music
making men's hearts thrill.
(*Church bells fade*)
Voices in the village street,
West Riding voices which I know
sound in a dull, uneven beat,
drum against my window-pane
muffled by hard-driven snow.

Frayne Ah do?

Narrator That was Tommy Frayne.

Crowe Nobbut middling.

Narrator Farmer Crowe
from Flower o' May, up Manor Lane –
even in paradise he'd complain.
I hear the roadman stamp his feet . . .
(*Stamp them*)
Sam's footsteps . . .
(*Slow, deliberate footsteps in snow passing*)
. . . firm, deliberate, slow.
(*Uncertain footsteps passing*)
Fred's – floppy as his old felt hat.

Matt (*calling*) I'll go and join them. Happy Noo Year, noo.

Narrator Matt. Old Matt –
taken by clods to be a clod
as he can neither read nor write.
Matt, earth-brown, hard-husked, kernel-sweet
as brown bread baked from stone-ground wheat.
Matt, who understood from birth
all living things born of the earth,
save men who swindle, twist and cod
and lie to neighbours as to God.
Matt, who made from the wild cherry
my white stick, my divining rod
to test man's mettle, hidden from sight.
(*A car and the lightning-quick blare of its horn*)

Driver (*That sort of driver, yelling*) Get out of my way!
(*The car passes . . .*)

Narrator A fool in a hurry.
(*. . . and crashes*)
I halt at the kerb, my heart's cage tight,
unable to look left or right.

Woman (*Courteous, correct compassion only*)
Can I help you?

Narrator Sightless or sighted, we are all blind –
but those who recognise
compassion in the voice of love
stand less in darkness and more in light.

Bibliography

Radio Plays

1947 THE PEACOCK CITY OF P'TZAN KING

1948 A SINGLE TAPER

THE INWARD EYE: BOY—1913

THE ISLAND OF WHITE BIRDS

1949 BARON BEAR AND THE LITTLE PRINCE, with Phyllis Scriven, in six parts

1950 POET AND ENGLISHMAN

LITTLE JAN PANDRUM, with Phyllis Scriven, in six parts

VI'LETS SWEET VI'LETS, with Phyllis Scriven

THE SNOW QUEEN, with Phyllis Scriven, in four parts

1951 ONE MAN'S CITY: LEEDS

1952 THE RUNAWAY ROCKING HORSE, with Phyllis Scriven

1953 BLUECAP AND THE SINGING WHEEL, with Phyllis Scriven

1954 JOY OF ANGELS

1955 THE NIGHT AND THE SHADOW

THE YEAR OF THE PHOENIX

1956 THE LAMP AND THE FLAME

1961 WRITING A PANTOMIME—THE BABES IN THE WOOD

1965 REYNARD THE FOX

1966 THE BLUE CLOAK

1968 JACK AND THE BEANSTALK

THE PROSPECT OF WHITBY

FIDDLER'S GREEN

THE SEASONS OF THE BLIND

1969 THE POLTERGOOSE

1970 ALL EARLY IN THE APRIL

THE PEACOCK SCREAMED ONE MORNING

1971 DANDELION AND PARSNIP: VINTAGE 1920

THE HOUSE OF HOUSES

1972 SUMMER WITH FLOWERS THAT FELL

1974 GIVE ME LONDON WEATHER, with Marc Scriven
A MEASURE OF SLIDING SAND

Published Works

1953 A SINGLE TAPER and THE INWARD EYE: BOY 1913, The Partridge Press
1959 THE YEAR OF THE PHOENIX AND OTHER POEMS: Secker & Warburg in association with The Partridge Press
1971 THE PROSPECT OF WHITBY, illustrated by Doreen Robert: Oxford University Press
1973 THE THINGUMMY JIG: Penguin Education
THE POLTERGOOSE: Penguin Education
1974 THE FAIRY TALE COOK BOOK: Eurobooks